The science fiction book

An illustrated history

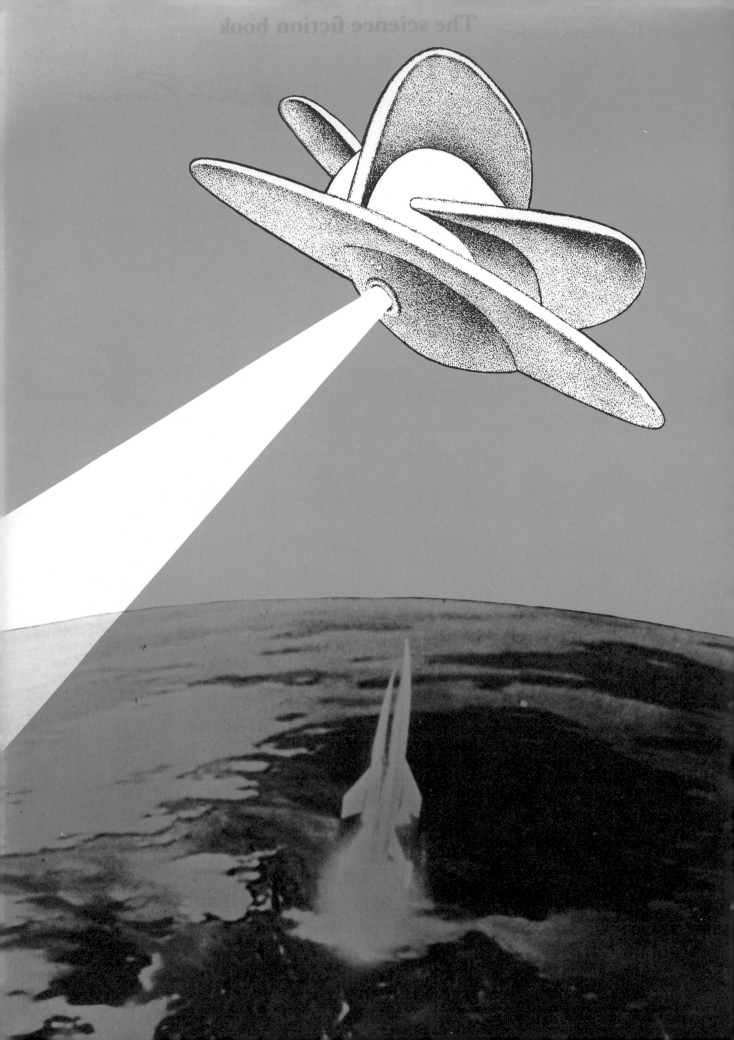

Franz Rottensteiner

THE SCIENCE FICTION BOOK

An illustrated history

NEW AMERICAN LIBRARY

TIMES MIRROR

NEW YORK AND SCARBOROUGH, ONTARIO

The author wishes to thank the following individuals and institutions for their kind help in the preparation of this book: Camille E. Cazedessus Jr, Prof. I. F. Clarke, Walter Ernsting, Heinz-Jürgen Ehrig, Kenneth W. Faig Jr, Charlotte Franke, Dan Fukami, Hal Hall, Dr Sándor Horvath, The Hungarian Art Foundation, Antal Jánosi, Prof. Michael Kandel, Peter Kuez, Dr Hans Langsteiner, Stanisław Lem, J. P. Moumon, Dr Josef Nesvadba, Emil Petaja, Petöfi Irodalmi Múzeum, Kazuya Sekita, Dr Margita Valehrachova, Riccard Valla, Donald A. Wollheim and Marek Wydmuch.

Library of Congress Catalog Card Number: 73-17886

ISBN: 0-8164-9169-0

SIGNET, SIGNET CLASSICS, MENTOR, PLUME and MERIDIAN BOOKS are published *in the United States* by The New American Library, Inc., 1301 Avenue of the Americas, New York, New York 10019, *in Canada* by The New American Library of Canada Limited, 81 Mack Avenue, Scarborough, 704, Ontario

PRINTED AND BOUND IN GREAT BRITAIN

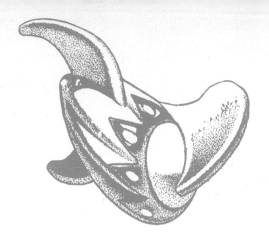

Contents

Introduction

Science fiction has seen a boom of unprecedented dimensions over the past few years. More sf books are being published all the time, in hardcover and in paperback, new works and reissues, novels and anthologies. Nor is this publishing explosion restricted to the U.S. and England; in fact it is virtually a world-wide phenomenon, its impact much the same in Germany, France, Italy, Hungary, Japan or the Soviet Union. Along with this flood of sf publications – only the magazines are stagnating – there is a growing interest in the discussion of science fiction, especially in academic circles. Since 1959 Wooster College, in Ohio, has been publishing *Extrapolation*, a scholarly periodical devoted to science fiction, edited by Professor Thomas D. Clareson; in Great Britain a similar publication, the *Foundation* journal, has been put out by the North-East London Polytechnic since 1972; and more recently there is *Science-Fiction Studies* published at Indiana State University, Terre Haute. Dozens of books on science fiction, both popular and scholarly, have appeared or are in preparation, in the U.S. and elsewhere. Several hundred courses on science fiction are being offered currently by American colleges, and seminars on science fiction have been offered periodically in other countries. The Clarion Writers' Workshop in Fantasy and Science Fiction, organized by Prof. Robin Scott Wilson of Clarion State College, has been a great success, and many of the Workshop students, taught by professional sf authors who function as visiting lecturers, have since been published professionally. Professor Wilson himself has put together three 'Clarion' anthologies (New American Library). As early as 1958 the Modern Language Association scheduled its first conference on science fiction, which has since become a regular affair. A 'Science Fiction Research Association' was formed in 1969, and various interdisciplinary conferences on 'Secondary Universes' have been organized by academic bodies. Apart from those scholarly events, there have been international science fiction symposia in Rio de Janeiro (1969), Tokyo (1970), and, for the science fiction circles of the socialist countries, Budapest (1971). A Festival of the Fantastic Film has been held annually in Trieste since 1963, and another similar festival was presented in Denmark in January 1973.

All these events (and the list could be expanded) testify to the growing interest in that elusive sphere known as 'science fiction.' But while the success of science fiction is evident, it is by no means clear what exactly science fiction is. Definitions are legion, and, as sf critic Damon Knight once remarked, trying to get two enthusiasts to agree on a definition of sf leads to bloody knuckles. Knight himself has defined science fiction as 'what we point to when we say it'; others claim that sf is everything that is offered by publishers under that name, while Brian W. Aldiss maintains that it doesn't exist. All extant definitions of course tend to include either too much or too little, but I have found three in particular to be useful for a first orientation in the field:

Science fiction is a branch of fantasy identifiable by the fact that it eases the 'willing suspension of disbelief' on the part of its readers by utilizing an atmos-

Virgil Finlay illustration for a story in Famous Fantastic Mysteries, *April 1950.*

phere of scientific credibility for its imaginative speculations in physical science, space, time, social science, and philosophy. (Science fiction historian Sam Moskowitz in *Seekers of Tomorrow*, Cleveland and New York, 1966.)

A science-fiction story is one which presupposes a technology, or an effect of technology, or a disturbance in the natural order, such as humanity, up to the time of writing, has not in actual fact experienced. (Edmund Crispin, *Best Science Fiction Stories*, London, 1955, p. 7)

Science Fiction is that class of prose narrative treating of a situation that could not arise in the world we know, but which is hypothesised on the basis of some innovation in science or technology, or pseudo-technology, whether human or extra-terrestrial in orgin. (Kingsley Amis, *New Maps of Hell*, London, 1960, p. 17)

Surprisingly popular is also the definition of the *good* science fiction story given by Theodore Sturgeon, a statement which is striking but also somewhat puzzling, since it strikes that author's own work from the field:

A science fiction story is a story built around human beings, with a human problem and a human solution, which would not have happened at all without its scientific content. (Quoted in James Blish's *The Issue at Hand*, Chicago, 1964, p. 14)

Even if we accept any one of these definitions, there is still ample doubt concerning the classification of individual works, not so much in terms of dividing science fiction from 'realistic' fiction as in separating sf from other kinds of fantasy, such as the traditional

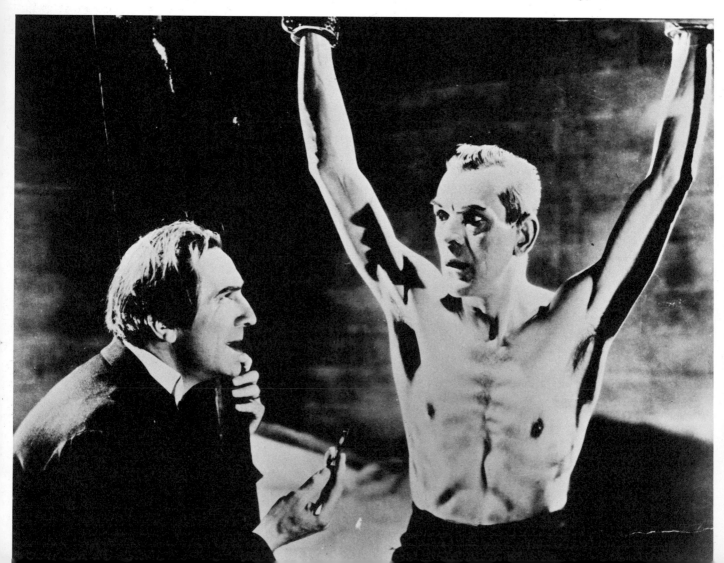

HAL YARROW   JEANNETTE   FOBO

Virgil Finlay illustration for The
Lovers *by Philip José Farmer, in*
Startling Stories, *August 1952. (See
also p. 118*)

*Bela Lugosi and Boris Karloff in a
still from* The Black Cat, *1934.*

fairy tale, weird fiction or 'light' fantasy. And while the trappings or the rationale behind science fiction may be different from those characterizing other fantasy, the fact that science fiction often appears side by side with the latter in the same magazines and books, that the audience is more or less the same, and that sf authors usually write all kinds of fantastic fiction, suggests that science fiction derives its psychic motivation from the sources that inspire all tales of the marvelous, all stories that refuse to be limited by what is possible in everyday life. This quality, a deep longing for the different, for 'otherness,' for a departure from the familiar norm, a desire to experience (if only in the mind) something unheard of, is what the initiated readers of science fiction like to call the 'sense of wonder': an ability to accept the radically different with an open mind, or to look at the familiar with a fresh eye, transforming it, as it were, into something strange and wonderful. This 'sense of wonder,' so often coupled with a child-like naiveté, may correspond to the *thaumazein* of the ancient Greeks which according to Aristotle is the beginning of all philosophy and hence all science. What in simple forms of science fiction may appear as simple-minded delight in the marvels of the universe, strangeness for the sake of strangeness, manifests itself in more sophisticated forms of sf as methodical doubt, the basis of scientific method.

For me, two stories have always exemplified the special pleasure to be gained from science fiction, although neither conforms to the concept of *science* fiction held by some older advocates and commonly known as 'Gernsback's delusion': that the task of

9

sf is to popularize science or to provide accurate technological prophecies. Indeed, in H. G. Wells's 'The Country of the Blind,' one of the two stories I have in mind, 'there are no scientific elements . . . and no obvious indulgence in fantasy at all' (Bernard Bergonzi, *The Early H. G. Wells*, Manchester, 1961, p. 78), and yet my own feeling that this story clearly belongs to science fiction is shared by at least one critic. See e.g., Robert M. Philmus, *Into the Unknown*, Berkeley and Los Angeles, 1970.

Why is this so? Wells's story, geographically located in a secluded valley, presents a closed 'world,' a model of another 'reality,' though one where the same physical laws apply as in our own world. Wells presents a world where all inhabitants are blind. The lone traveler who stumbles upon the valley of the blind literally enters another world, and far from becoming the king of the proverb, he is an anomaly, severely handicapped by his distinguishing advantage, his sense of sight. In several respects, 'The Country of the Blind' embodies the method of science fiction. It takes an abstract idea (in this case a generally accepted sentence) and turns it into 'concrete myth' (Philmus). And Wells not only concretizes the idea, but proceeds to throw doubt upon it and provide an ironic commentary on it. That's not all there is to the story, either; metaphorically it is as meaningful as it is when taken literally, for the hero of the story is 'the man who sees among those who do not see, the open mind among the conformists, a free spirit in a bourgeois world' (Bergonzi, p. 80).

A more recent pendant to Wells's story is Isaac Asimov's 'Nightfall.' Like

'The Country of the Blind,' it takes the 'metaphoric substance of an idea' (Philmus, p. 21), inverts it, and provides it with flesh in a story: 'If the stars should appear one night in a thousand years, how would men believe and adore, and preserve for many generations the remembrance of the city of God!' (Emerson). Unlike Emerson, Asimov undertakes to show that such an event, far from inspiring any awe of the star-sprinkled sky, would result in panic and disorder, leading to a cataclysm that periodically wipes out civilization on another planet. Following the usage of science fiction, and the logical necessity of the situation, Asimov has located his story in another star system, but otherwise he follows Wells's plan on another scale: he builds the fictional model of a closed system, where universal physical laws are the same as the laws we know, but certain astronomic specifics are different; and these specifics have consequences that set the inhabitants of this world apart from us psychologically in so far as they have never seen the stars. Like the tale by Wells, 'Nightfall' allows both literal and metaphorical

interpretation, and the latter shows that the story's emotional content is basically antirationalistic: the catastrophic emergence of the starry sky might be interpreted as symbolic of enlightenment, that not only a little knowledge is a dangerous thing, but too much knowledge as well; and that revolution, or too much of a new condition, leads inevitably to the downfall of civilization. The human beings presented in 'Nightfall' are as blind to one essential characteristic of their world as are the people in 'The Country of the Blind,' and when the true nature of their world is revealed to them, they flee into madness. In some respects the story is a sf translation of Plato's famous cave parable.

Saul Bellow (in *Mr Sammler's Planet*) has called 'The Country of the Blind' a 'bad story,' and considered purely as a piece of fiction 'Nightfall' is even worse, which makes it all the more representative of science fiction, for it must be admitted that many works in the field (including stories considered to be of 'classic' stature) are aesthetically inferior products. Nevertheless, flat as the descriptions in 'Nightfall' are, predictable though the plot may be, and as second-hand as the whole thing is (for the basic idea was given young Isaac Asimov by editor John W. Campbell, Jr in whose magazine the story first appeared), the story has considerable impact – an impact that is derived wholly from extraliterary factors. 'Nightfall' transmits a sense of new perceptions opened, a view of a potentially grandiose world, almost like the 'oceanic feeling' of Romain Rolland, akin to myth and religious awe. In his book *Of Other Worlds* (London, 1966, p. 16) C. S. Lewis rejected a religious interpretation of sf advanced by Roger Lancelyn Green, adding: 'If he had said simply that something which the educated receive from poetry can reach the masses through stories of adventure, and almost in no other way, then I think he would have been right.' Lewis's statement points to the paradoxical nature of science fiction as that which contains something akin to poetry, and yet set apart from it by an aesthetic deficit. This longing for poetry in science fiction (as expressed in many reviews) is only surpassed by a prevalent taste for bad poetry, much as the enthusiasm for science among many sf writers is often over-ridden by their ignorance of it. In my opinion, science fiction is best described by such paradoxes, by the deep desire for the unattainable, only natural in a field of writing where ambition and publicly proclaimed aims so often exceed real potential and abilities.

Since the beginning, two conflicting attitudes have been interwoven in sf writing. On the one hand there is the grandeur of horizons that have ex-

panded to encompass the whole universe (or even other universes as well), and the insignificance of the human microbes inhabiting this gigantic cosmos. Occasionally mankind is even seen as the cancer and the vermin of the universe, a contemptible species to be ignored, exterminated (as in Thomas M. Disch's novel *The Genocides*), or kept as the pets or the cattle of some extraterrestrial race. On the other hand there is a fierce pride in the ability of these human microbes to understand the universe, and to become masters of it, either conceptually through the development of hypotheses and theories or, more often, by conquering it physically. In some cases the sense of pride leads us to conceive that mankind will outlive the physical universe (i.e., 'our' physical universe), as in James Blish's *A Clash of Cymbals* or Poul Anderson's *Tau Zero*. These conflicting possibilities are either presented as simply an exercise in imagining other conditions, without passing judgment on them, or they are given emotional color – either embraced with longing or, conversely, rejected with abhorrence and held out as a warning. Even more common is an uneasy mixture of those elements, as often as not motivated by hidden impulses that may be at cross-purposes with the author's stated aim. Because of such conflicting and diffuse attitudes, science fiction is often censored as being unrelievedly gloomy, or, alternatively, is blamed for a naive and superficial optimism. In recent years the war between the 'optimists' and the 'pessimists' in Anglo-American science fiction has been waged between the defenders of older science fiction and the proponents of the 'New Wave,' who,

some older writers feel, pose a danger to the genre and offer a degrading picture of human nature. The underlying assumptions of 'positive' and 'negative' thinking, common as they are in human history, have of course always been present in science fiction, as well as throughout its prehistory. Nor are individual writers free of oscillations between those extremes. Even the supremely optimistic Jules Verne wrote the stark story 'The New Adam,' and in H. G. Wells the utopian hope for a brighter future wrestles with the fear that the future may be more hell than paradise. These two poles, the dimension of hope and the fear and abhorrence of its opposite, are equally important in science fiction, which is only to be expected, for it hardly seems possible to pledge a whole literary form to a single outlook, let alone a form as heterogeneous as science fiction, which seems so singularly destined to throw doubt on existing conditions by presenting or implying alternatives.

Modern science fiction is a mixed genre that has derived its concepts, story patterns and techniques from many sources, both literary and non-literary, and has transposed and assimilated them to such an extent that it is difficult to tell what is 'pure' science fiction, and what is 'contamination' or 'loan genre' (e.g. the Western or war story simply dislocated into the future). Often mistaken for a typical American phenomenon, the currently prevalent view is that science fiction as we know it today got its start with the first issue of *Amazing Stories* in April 1926, although the term itself wasn't coined until three years later by the same Hugo Gernsback who founded *Amazing*

Illustration by the Hungarian artist Hegedüs István for a novel by Stanisław Lem. (See also pp. 148–149)

12

Stories. According to this view, the year 1926 was a decisive caesura, and science fiction was something new under the sun. One sf author, Cyril M. Kornbluth, has denounced all attempts to unearth old examples of 'science fiction,' though many histories date science fiction as far back as Lucian of Samosata, Aristophanes and Plato. This last method is as dubious as the one which gives a precise date for the 'birth' of a new literary genre. Less open to attack is the position somewhere in between, that, although science fiction, like any other genre, had its forerunners, it originated as a separate category in the second half of the nineteenth century or around the turn of the century. Stories of the type presented in *Amazing Stories* had been written for decades and longer; one American study, Bruce H. Franklin's *Future Perfect* (New York, 1966), claims that 'there was no major nineteenth-century American writer of fiction, and indeed few in the second rank, who did not write some science fiction or at least one utopian romance.' Much the same could be shown for certain other countries, at least in terms of the quantity of science fiction, if not its quality.

All this notwithstanding, there is much to be said for the view that dates the beginning of modern science fiction at the emergence of *Amazing Stories*, not for any immediate literary effect or novelty the magazine may have offered, but for the social consequences of this concentration of speculative fiction in one single publication. Up to then, 'scientific fiction,' 'future fiction,' 'scientific romances,' or 'anticipatory tales' had been published only in books, in general magazines along with other

An example of 'underground comix' from a German magazine, Science Fiction Times, *November-December 1972. (See also illustration on p. 22)*

A still from Stanley Kubrick's film Dr. Strangelove, *in which the destruction of the world was predicted.*

types of fiction, or in a few 'dime novels' featuring a series hero; and there was continuity only in the latter. What *Amazing Stories* did provide was a focus, a rallying point for all the people interested in this kind of thing, and it did that when the time was ripe, when the progress of science and the increase of literacy had created a large enough potential audience. From a number of isolated works written by authors who had to compete with all kinds of fiction, and who drew their inspiration from the fabric of life around them rather than from the old tomes that scholars have declared to be early science fiction, science fiction gradually became concentrated in a number of specialized publications – 'the sf field,' originally magazines, but then increasingly in pocket-book form.

The consequences of this development (both positive and negative) are well known. Whereas formerly sf writers had to keep their place among writers of general fiction – called 'the mainstream' in science fictionese – it was now possible for them to specialize in speculations about the future, to write things that

would have seemed utterly ridiculous in any other environment, and to reap praise from a readership equally specialized in the fantastic. While the quality of books is not necessarily higher than that of magazines, the magazines provide the sort of continuity of tradition that tends to keep clichés alive, transmitting them from story to story and from writer to writer. The confinement to specialized magazines made possible easy dismissal by the public based on generic rather than individual criteria, or sometimes on mere prejudice and ignorance. On the other hand, it furthered identification for the avid readers of the fantastic, and their formation into groups in close contact with the producers of science fiction – a phenomenon unique to science fiction, then as now. It also increased the defensive tendency, always strong among the more enthusiastic, often missionary-minded 'fans' of science fiction, to counter the general contempt prompted by lurid covers and a mass of drivel, by proclaiming sf as something special, a genre apart from the rest of literature, and therefore to be measured by stan-

dards having no relationship with anything to be found in general literary criticism. Thus even if sf was admittedly 'bad' from a literary point of view, it was said to possess some unique virtue that made the question of literary value meaningless. For instance, at the Third Annual Science Fiction Convention (1941) in Denver, Colorado, popular sf writer Robert A. Heinlein declared in his speech 'The Discovery of the Future': 'I think that science fiction, even the corniest of it, even the most outlandish of it, no matter how badly it's written, has a distinct therapeutic value because *all* of it has as its primary postulate that the world does *change*.' Since then, many other sf writers have upheld this creed of change as the raison d'être of science fiction, even where claims to prophecy were rejected. Interestingly enough, most changes in the arsenal of science fiction are of the sort that nobody, not even the most conservative man, need fear he will ever have to undergo: the emergence of telepathic supermen, time travel, feudal future societies, psi phenomena, invasions from space and so on, while the more urgent and imminent changes that will surely affect our future lives are often ignored. Nor does the violence with which changes in science fiction itself are 'welcomed' (as in the war against the 'New Wave' of some years back), the literary conservatism of so much of it, particularly suggest that readers of science fiction are better equipped to face the future than non-readers of it. What Karl R. Popper, in *The Poverty of Historicism* (New York, 1964), said about this doctrine may well be applied to science fiction.

Modern historicists, however, seem to be

unaware of the antiquity of their doctrine. They believe – and what else could their deification of modernism permit? – that their own brand of historicism is the latest and boldest achievement of the human mind, an achievement so staggeringly novel that only a few people are sufficiently advanced to grasp it. They believe, indeed, that it is they who have discovered the problem of change – one of the oldest problems of speculative metaphysics.

Contrasting their 'dynamic' thinking with the 'static' thinking of all previous generations, they believe that we are now 'living in a revolution' which has so much accelerated the speed of our development that social change can now be directly experienced within a single lifetime. Important revolutions have occurred before our time, and since the days of Heraclitus change has been discovered over and over again.

To present so venerable an idea as bold and revolutionary is, I think, to betray an unconscious conservatism.' (pp. 160–61)

Rather than being of therapeutic value or offering a life philosophy, the concept of change in science fiction often turns into a fixed formula, a jumble of fantastic changes. This may indeed be an inevitable result of the particular method of

A monster portrayed by the 19th-century artist, Gustave Doré.

Illustration by Hannes Bok for a special edition (1946) of Abraham Merritt's The Fox Woman. *The illustration on p. 4 is from the same publication.*

HANNES BOK 1946

science fiction, the mixture and composition of disparate and even incongruous elements. The rules that govern the process of juxtaposing various building blocks, as it were, in the edifice of sf works, are well summarized in a passage in David Hume's *Inquiry Concerning Human Understanding*:

What never was seen, or heard of, may yet be conceived; nor is any thing beyond the power of thought, except what implies an absolute contradiction.

But though our thought seems to possess this unbounded liberty, we shall find, upon a nearer examination, that it is really confined within very narrow limits, and that all this creative power of the mind amounts to no more than the faculty of compounding, transposing, augmenting, or diminishing the materials afforded us by the senses and experience.

Science fiction takes pride in its freedom from restrictions, in the novelty and boldness of its concepts; and yet, upon closer examination, we may simply unearth a few basic notions, varied and elaborated upon in scores of stories. By refusing to acknowledge limits – true, not unconditional and ever-changing limits – science fiction attains a false feeling of freedom that is not based on a careful examination of its premises but rather has its foundation in philosophical naiveté, and which is the reason for the intellectual and emotional immaturity of so much of it. Such diverse critics of science fiction as Arthur Koestler, Michel Butor and Stanislaw Lem agree that this boundless fantastic roaming about is a weakness of sf rather than a strength. 'Nothing, at first view, may seem more unbounded than the thought of man; which not only escapes all human power and authority, but is not even restrained within the limits of nature and reality. To form monsters, and join incongruous shapes and appearances, costs the imagination no more trouble than to conceive the most natural and familiar objects' (David Hume). The sf imagination is the kind that refuses to recognize limits, and offers a gigantic bestiary encompassing time and space. It links familiar ideas, such as (in Hume's example) the ideas of gold and mountains, to form the unfamiliar (a golden mountain). Human beings are turned into giants or dwarves, sometimes even reduced to the size of atoms, or crossbred with various animal shapes. On other planets we re-encounter the fauna and flora of Earth, either untransposed or combined in fantastic arrangements. Among the galaxies the Roman Empire rises again, fantastically enlarged, destined once more to decline and fall; feudalism is reborn among the stars or on a future Earth, and the Stone Age returns after an atomic war on another planet. Or the hero is transported by his time machine so that the most amazingly computerized future meets the remotest past. Nothing is ever really lost in the dim reaches of history, there are no irreversible developments: past, present and future coexist in one all-encompassing continuum; what has ever been crops up again in the future, along with some things that never were, will not and cannot be.

To be true to its credo, to justify its existence, science fiction should ideally concentrate on the absolutely novel. But such a task would require a breadth and profundity of intellect beyond that of any conceivable practitioner; and

this lack has led to the present state of science fiction, which features 'change' in terms of any past contrasted with the present, and jazzed up by super-scientific detail. The large mass of science fiction is a synchronous, ahistorical literature that mixes elements from the past without regard for their proper historical contexts, although often with pseudo-historical trappings, and sometimes even with the moral of 'historical parallel' spelled out at great length for a readership untrained in the subtleties of literary exposition. A literature of vast assimilative powers, science fiction has been able to absorb elements from many literary genres and to make them its own. At the same time, sf has never become the legitimate heir to these genres, most of which still have an independent life of their own, although some have disappeared for all practical purposes, confined as they were to particular eras of literary history.

Most prominent of the latter group is of course the literary utopia, the genre that derived its name from Thomas More's tale of that title. German scholars such as Schwonke and Krysmanski – who take their science fiction more philosophically than most – have interpreted sf as the legitimate contemporary form of utopian thinking. Whereas older utopias drew blueprints for Eden, and thus advocated one specific brand of change – that towards the improvement of social conditions on Earth – science fiction tries to present all kinds of temporary changes, good, bad, and indifferent. It tries to be prepared not just for one specific future, but for all kinds of possible and impossible futures. As Schwonke puts it, the engineer of a better future turns into

the chief of staff preparing for all contingencies that might arise in the future. According to this view, which was strongly influenced by the thinking of Raymond Ruyer, sf would be defined as the intellectual art of developing speculative models of different worlds, a philosophy of *Als Ob* (As If), without passing judgment on the desirability of those worlds. This notion is acceptable as an ideal of what science fiction could and perhaps should do, but it is hardly borne out by the present state of the genre, for the majority of the models presented by science fiction are too vague and superficial to be compared to the precision of the speculative models presented by futurology and other scientific disciplines. Much of science fiction has fallen far behind the classical utopias; nevertheless, something of utopia lives on in science fiction, even something of utopian hope, and the more this holds, the better a work of sf usually is.

More alive today is the imaginary voyage, which is rarely treated outside of science fiction, as opposed to the occasional utopia that turns up in the work of some mainstream author not connected with science fiction. Voyages of discovery, quests among the stars, odysseys on other planets hold a strong appeal in science fiction. Alien planets, stars and galaxies are full of marvels, unknown species and communities to be discovered, and social aspects necessarily enter there, for the intelligent beings discovered are bound to have some sort of social organization. Occasionally the mores of these peoples are conceived as a distorting mirror of human affairs, but more often science fiction is interested in them not as a

reflection, but for the value they have in themselves: either out of a near-scientific curiosity in the possible, or simply from the kind of idle interest provided by two-headed calves. From *Robinson Crusoe* derives the pattern of the shipwrecked man, the story of the individual or group pitted in a game of wits against a hostile environment, with no other resources than their brains. Examples of sf 'robinsonades' are Rex Gordon's *First on Mars*, John W. Campbell's *The Moon Is Hell* or Tom Godwin's *The Survivors*.

Mary W. Shelley's *The Last Man* (1826) prefigured one of the more popular sf themes, especially with British writers: the world catastrophe that wipes out most of mankind. In George R. Stewart's *Earth Abides*, the cataclysmic novel achieved remarkable literary heights. The world cataclysm is a theme most acceptable to the general reader, not requiring him to adapt to outlandish concepts and contraptions; and from the author it demands only the traditional literary skill in the description of human beings in an extreme situation.

Famine, floods, the ravages of war, plagues – those are misfortunes that anybody can imagine happening to him, thus establishing easy identification.

Many of the dominant narrative patterns of science fiction have been supplied by popular fiction, including the historical novel, the adventure story, the war novel, the nurse story, the love romance, the sea story, the mystery and even the Western – as in *Six-Gun Planet* by John Jakes, *A Planet for Texans* by H. Beam Piper and John J. McGuire or *Planet Run* by Keith

Laumer and Gordon R. Dickson; many other stories have adopted the pattern of the Western without acknowledging it openly. Especially close ties exist between sf and the mystery novel. The question has been asked whether it is possible successfully to mix sf and the mystery in a viable hybrid; yet sf itself is a mixed form which has derived its patterns from so many genres that it would be difficult to explain which are the 'pure' sf structures. Although occasionally one can hear talk of 'science-fiction techniques,' there exists

Scene from the Paramount sf film, When Worlds Collide (*1951*), *based on a novel by Edwin Balmer and Philip Wylie.*

no single study that attempts to show precisely what those techniques are, and to prove that they are unique to sf. What Damon Knight calls 'the kitchen-sink story,' for instance, seems to be merely an elaboration upon the 'universal processes' described by David Hume, a story into which the author throws any ideas that may occur to him, in the desperate hope that quantity will in some miraculous way turn into quality. It is a sort of notional saturation bombing, based on the pious hope of achieving some hits. The results of this method may be seen in the work of A. E. van Vogt, for one.

Another major influence on science fiction has been the Gothic novel. Mary W. Shelley's *Frankenstein* supplied the pattern of the creature who turns against its creator and the scientist who is punished for playing God. *Frankenstein* presented the dark side of science, or rather, it recast the setting

of scientific investigation with an older myth alien to science: that knowledge is evil, and that the 'Modern Prometheus' consequently must pay the price for his presumption. This pattern was dominant in the early years of *Amazing Stories*, when editorials stressed the educational and scientific value of science fiction, and the scientific creed was proclaimed more loudly than at any time in the history of sf, while the stories printed in the same magazine indicated the horrible consequences of that creed.

The scientific horror pattern was firmly established by Edgar Allan Poe, one of the most important forerunners of science fiction. Poe often provided 'verisimilitude' in the form of long verbatim quotes lifted liberally and without acknowledgment from contemporary scientific sources. Interested in the dark sides of human nature, he turned to such border sciences as mesmerism to support the fantastic events in his stories. Science fiction has followed him in this by providing a home for occult lore, embracing as it does the whole body of psi-phenomena and the science of parapsychology.

As a rule, sf has always found it easier to assimilate fictional science – from the 'hollow earth' theory of Captain Symmes to visions of Atlantis, the collections of Charles Fort, and the Dianetics/Scientology propounded by sf author L. Ron Hubbard – than to embody in its structure actual scientific hypotheses. And even where real science does enter sf, it may be distorted or simplified in order to better serve narrative purposes.

Yet although the 'science' of science fiction is often undistinguishable from magic – and there are sf myths with a base of technological rationalization – there is a fundamental difference between science fiction and supernatural horror stories or straight fantasy. This difference lies in the formal relationship to natural law. Science fiction assumes implicitly (and often explicitly) that everything in the universe can be explained by natural law, although the definition of 'natural law' may foreshadow some actual future development of science; or conversely, may be based on an imperfect understanding (or total misunderstanding) of science. What is important, though, is that sf authors may bend natural law, but will never break it; they cannot dispense with the prestigious name of 'science,' dominated by scientific thinking as our age is. C. S. Lewis clearly recognized this in his elegant reply to J. B. S. Haldane's criticism of his novel *That Hideous Strength*: 'Every tyrant must begin by claiming to have what his victims respect and give what they want. The majority of people in modern countries respect science and want to be planned. And, therefore, almost by definition, if any man or group wishes to enslave us it will of course describe itself as "scientific planned democracy"' (*Of Other Worlds*, London, 1966, p. 80). Thus sf invites its authors to take up the cloak of science with which they can dignify all the magic, occult lore, fairy tales and myths of old.

Fantasy, on the other hand, either offers a co-universe, ruled by laws openly presented as magical (as in the stories printed in magazines such as *Unknown* or the 'Adult Fantasy' published in the Ballantine series of that name) – in other words, fairy tales for

(*Above*) *A still of the 1920 film version of* Dr. Jekyll and Mr. Hyde (*Paramount Pictures Corp.*).

(*Opposite*) *The ubiquitous Virgil Finlay, this time illustrating the seminal H. G. Wells novel,* The Time Machine, *reprinted in* Famous Fantastic Mysteries, *August 1950.*

grown-ups; or, as horror fantasy, it presents 'a break' (Roger Caillois), a disturbance in the fabric of the universe, a suspension of natural law (indeed the most horrible thing we can imagc). Or, as Ray Bradbury once put it: science fiction keeps us suspended; fantasy shoves us over the cliff.

The border between the two worlds is not clearly defined, however. H. P. Lovecraft, a writer much influenced by Poe, presented in many of his stories a universe peopled by horrors living on distant stars; yet his creations may or may not transgress natural law, and at least several of his stories ('The Shadow Out of Time', 'The Color Out of Space') are clearly science fiction. Some sf stories, such as James Blish's 'There Shall Be No Darkness,' have made use of a more traditional arsenal of fantastic beings (werewolves, in the case of Blish's story) and attempt to give a 'scientific' explanation for them. Tales like this are good examples for the eclecticism of sf. Curiously enough, by supplying a 'rational' interpretation of fantastic happenings, they sacrifice the emotional, truly horrifying basis of such stories (their irrationality and inexplicability) for the solution of a puzzle, an exercise of the ratiocinating faculties of the mind. Other themes from traditional fantasy, particularly that of the Protean monster, have been skilfully adopted by sf (e.g., John W. Campbell's 'Who Goes There?'). And it is indicative of the ambivalent mood of science fiction that this theme also finds its opposite pole: in Damon Knight's 'Four in One' humans joyfully become part of a Protean creature.

Many sf methods can be readily studied in Jules Verne, who is together

with Wells the most important representative of the genre before its official emergence as a 'field.' Verne was much influenced by Poe, from whom he lifted some plot elements, and whose *Narrative of Arthur Gordon Pym* Verne continued in *The Ice Sphinx*: but more important was the practice of giving scientific verisimilitude to his stories by bolstering them with data lifted from the scientific publications of his day; what Poe had done secretly, Verne turned into an open virtue, freely acknowledging his sources to stress the authenticity of his novels. Quite modest in his technological forecasting, careful to present only inventions that already existed at least in blueprint form, Verne was a timid extrapolator who never stepped beyond the body of accepted fact and theory; and indeed, only in a very few stories did he venture toward other planets or into the future. Rather, his novels explored Earth, mapping it as it were in his fiction.

Jules Verne might be called the Linnaeus of science fiction, the industrious cataloger of facts, and up to the present much of science fiction, especially in American novel-length sf, has followed his tradition, although his cautious attitude abouts facts has long been discarded. Science fiction is no longer tied to Earth, but fills the whole universe with the stuff of marvels. Similarly, extrapolation ranges far into the future, with authors often making up their own laws of physics. Modern authors still share Verne's delight in 'facts,' however, and this predilection for numbers and figures (preferably

Scene from the 1925 film version of The Lost World, *based on Conan Doyle's novel. (See pp. 84–87)*

those with a sufficiently impressive number of zeros). Today as in Verne's heyday, the typical sf hero is generally a lone being, cut off from the rest of society; in modern sf, this difference is often indicated by superhuman 'talents' that set him apart from his fellow men: extra-sensory powers, eidetic memory, unusual physical strength, superhuman speed and agility. Such 'mutants' are invariably the result of natural evolution, often caused by radiation, in the wake of an atomic war, say. As Michel Butor has pointed out, Verne attributed mystical significance to many places on Earth: the poles, the center of the Earth and so on; and to 'be the first there' was of tremendous importance for his heroes; today's sf is also concerned with the sensational, the record-making effort, and seeks the 'meaning of the universe' as something to be found out among the stars rather than arrived at by introspection and reflection.

Quite different is the sf of H. G. Wells, although he too wrote his share of stories that merely feature new inventions, such as 'The Land Ironclads.' By design and in principle Wells created stories that were far more philosophical in content than those of Verne. It is in the short story field that the Wellsian tradition is most alive in sf today. Science fiction has achieved its most impressive results when it has focused on no more than a few ideas, and explored the meaning and the consequences of those ideas. Examples of this kind of story are Daniel Keyes's 'Flowers for Algernon,' Damon Knight's 'The Country of the Kind' (with its punning reference to Wells in the title), Fritz Leiber's 'Coming Attractions,' Henry Kuttner's 'Mimsy

Were the Borogroves' or Cyril M. Kornbluth's 'The Altar at Midnight.'

An ideal science fiction – one to be taken seriously from both an artistic and an intellectual point of view – would combine the best features of Verne and Wells: careful attention to facts, inspired by bold speculation. Scrupulous in detail without getting bogged down in data, and relating these to the whole of human existence, it would ride through the high adventure of the inquisitive spirit, explore really new possibilities, other states of being, alternatives, and embody the critical method of science and philosophy in symbolical narrative. That a science fiction is in fact possible that takes its science seriously and contains speculations of a high intellectual order is demonstrated by the work of the Pole Stanislaw Lem. If Verne was the Linnaeus of science fiction, then perhaps Lem is its Darwin, a *homo theoreticus* of the first order.

Needless to say, the ideal of intellectual brilliance and consummate stylistic artistry is rarely attained in science fiction. Yet even in its imperfect form, the *ars combinatoria* that is modern science fiction, this 'modern mythology' of old and new elements, is an impressive testimony to the ability of the human mind to go beyond mere empiricism. Thus this book is offered as an introduction to the many worlds of science fiction, a guided tour through strange territory, and should the reader be moved to forge further into those realms, it will have served its purpose. Sf today is far more than simply stories of space travel (the theme the general public most often associates with the genre). It offers a look into the whole

universe and into ourselves, a kaleidoscope of glimpses into the space-time continuum, combining the comfort of familiarity with the excitement of novelty. Whether it primarily serves to impart technological or scientific data, whether escape entertainment or food for critical thought, sf always plays the fabulous game of 'What if?', a challenge to the mental faculties of its readers. Therein lie its justification and its value.

(Overleaf) Looking out into the Future: a still from the film version of H. G. Wells's Things to Come.

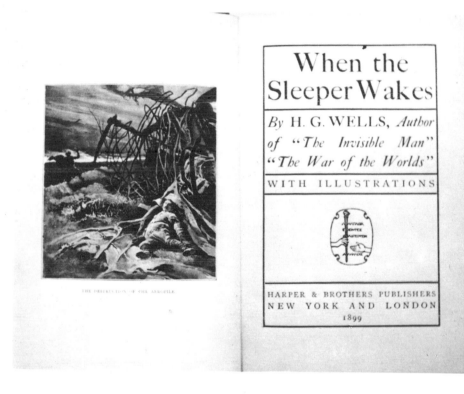

(*Left*) *An illustration* (*by Almos Zaschik*) *in the Hungarian edition of Wells's* The Time Machine. (*Above*) *The frontispiece and title page of* When the Sleeper Wakes, *and the cover illustration on the Turkish translation of* The Time Machine.

In novels like *The Time Machine* (1895), *The Island of Dr. Moreau* (1896), *The Invisible Man* (1897), *When the Sleeper Wakes* (1899), *The First Men in the Moon* (1904), and in short stories such as 'The Flowering of the Strange Orchid', 'The Lord of the Dynamos', 'The Star' or 'The New Accelerator', H. G. Wells presented virtually every idea that has since become common stock in science fiction, and nobody in the field has ever surpassed his work – which speaks as much for Wells's reputation as against those to come after him.

Wells was born in 1866, the son of an unsuccessful salesman; he escaped from being a draper's apprentice, studied science under T. H. Huxley, took up teaching, and later became a journalist and a writer. His later books, both fiction and nonfiction, took up 'great causes,' and he explicitly denied any desire to write literature, calling himself a journalist. Whatever one may think of his later work, his early stories were subtly polished works of art which also knew how to entertain. He is marvelously complex and deeply symbolic, particularly in *The Time Machine*, an introduction to one theme which has by now become a sf cliché. But whereas modern authors are interested in time travel for its own sake, in the paradoxes and complications resulting from it ('What if you went back in time and killed your own grandfather before he had time to beget your father?'), Wells used time travel primarily as a literary device, a method to transport his

27

(*Above*) *Rod Taylor at the controls: a clip from the Hollywood film of* The Time Machine. (*Opposite*) *Before the blast-off: Alexander Korda's production of* Things to Come.

(*Below*) *Another Virgil Finlay illustration for the sf magazine reprint of* The Time Machine.

narrator into a strange future – the world of 802,701. Man has become separated into two distinct species, the Eloi and the Morlocks. Whereas the Eloi, small, beautiful and childlike beings, live on the surface of the Earth in a veritable Eden, the ugly misshapen Morlocks, their darker brothers, toil in the dreaded, dark underworld. After the idyllic Arcadia of the first half of the story, the traveler descends into the labyrinths of the demoniac Morlocks – who are not, as he had first assumed, the slaves of the Eloi, but rather prey on them, quite literally, for they are carnivorous. The story poetically incorporates many evolutionary ideas, and also a few Marxist themes, such as the division between the ruling and working classes, a gulf here seen as unbridgeable and indeed built into the race. This ambiguous attitude, the extrapolation of what science can do in the future, and an uneasy feeling about the consequences of those achievements mark Wells's early scientific romances, and it is this brilliantly critical method that raises his symbolical narratives far above those of his contemporary, Jules Verne, of whom Wells rightly said:

These tales have been compared with the work of Jules Verne and there was a disposition on the part of literary journalists at one time to call me the English Jules Verne. As a matter of fact there is no literary resemblance whatever between the anticipatory inventions of the great Frenchman and these fantasies. His work dealt almost always with actual possibilities of invention and discovery, and he made some remarkable forecasts. The interest he evoked was a practical one; he wrote and believed that this or that thing could be done, which was not at that time done. He helped his reader to imagine it being done and to realize what fun, excitement or mischief would ensue. Most of his inventions have 'come true'. But these stories of mine . . . do not pretend to deal with possible things, they are exercises of the imagination in a quite different field. They belong to a class of writing which includes the Golden Ass of Apuleius, the True Histories of Lucian, Peter Schlemihl, and the story of Frankenstein.

29

Fantasies of flight

In 1648, Bishop John Wilkins wrote in his *Mathematical Magick*:

There are four several ways whereby this flying in air hath been or may be attempted. Two of them by the strength of other things, and two of them by our own strength. 1 By spirits, or angels. 2 By the help of fowls. 3 By wings fastened immediately to the body. 4 By a flying chariot.

The desire to fly, to see the earth with a bird's eye, is as old as mankind, and proto-science fiction has employed all the forms described by Bishop Wilkins. The myth of Dedalus and Icarus is only one expression of this dream. 'To get wings and make a journey into heaven,' is the desire of Lucian's Menippus in *Icaromennipus*, one of the earliest accounts of a fantastic voyage beyond the Earth (wings for man are also featured in Lucian's other romance, the *True History*). Alexander the Great is also said to have made an attempt at the heavens 'and see if they be the heaven which we behold.' But some divine intervention brought down his gryphons, and once more the mighty had fallen.

One of the strangest novels of flight is *La Découverte australe Par un Homme-volant, ou la Dédale français* (Paris, 1871), written by Restif de la Bretonne, who is better known as a pornographer than as a Utopian. Bretonne's hero Victorin is not so much interested in furthering science as in exploring far regions of this earth, and even the moon and the planets. Violently in love with a lady from a higher social class, he makes himself a pair of artificial wings and carries off his beloved to an inaccessible mount where they lead a

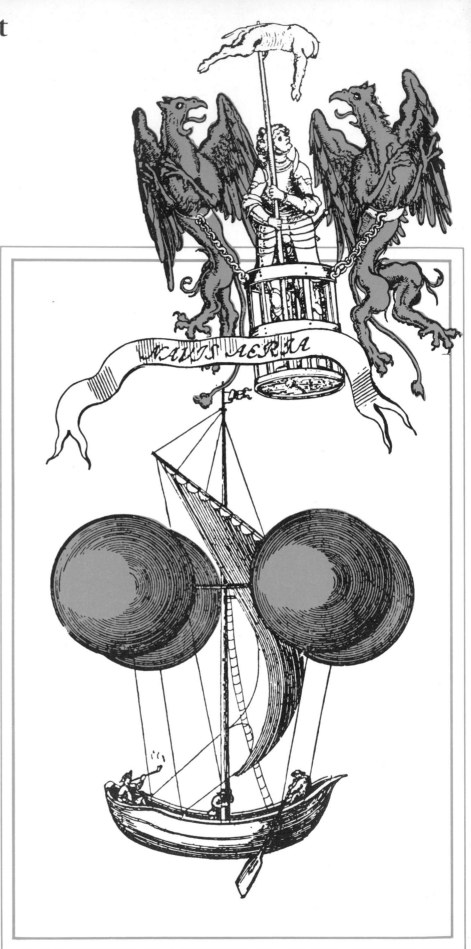

(Opposite, above) Alexander the Great borne into space by two griffins in a wood engraving by Hans Leonhard Schaüffelein (16th century). (Below) A flying machine, its crew and passengers (one of them obviously an early victim of travel-sickness) in Bernard Zamagna's Navis Aerea. (Right) Illustration from Die geschwinde Reise. (Below right) A space ship illustrated in Laurenco de Gusmão's Passarola (1709). (Below, left) Cover illustration to Restif de la Bretonne's La Découverte australe (1871).

natural but interesting life, flying over many countries and begetting flying children.

Modern rocketry in sf can be said to begin with Verne's *From the Earth to the Moon*, even though he employed a space gun, and rockets were used only for the navigation of his projectile in space. Since Verne's time sf has produced a large variety of space drives. Even after the first sputnik was launched in 1957, which a large section of the reading public interpreted as proof that science had finally 'caught up' with sf, space travel and the exploration of other worlds have remained the one theme most easily identified with sf, and the rocket-ship is still its most familiar symbol.

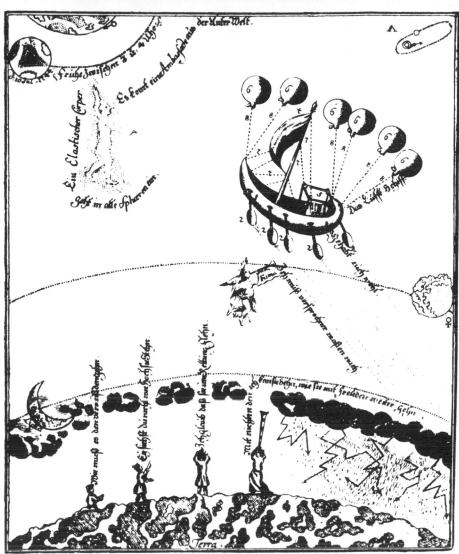

The modern Prometheus: Frankenstein, Mr Hyde, Dr Moreau

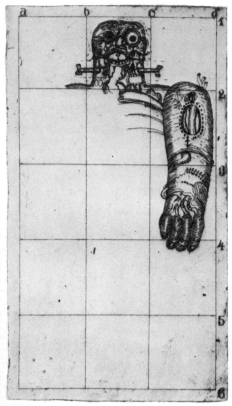

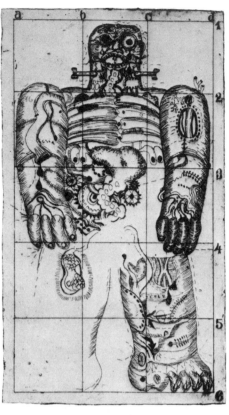

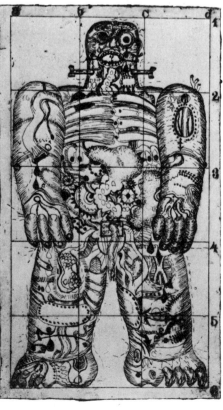

In 1818, Mary Wollstonecraft Shelley (1797–1851), wife of the poet, published *Frankenstein, or, The Modern Prometheus.* The origins of this tale of terror, written when Mary Shelley was only nineteen, date back to the summer of 1816, when Mary, her future husband, Lord Byron and Byron's physician William Polidori were staying at the Villa Diodati near Geneva. Having read some German ghost stories, the company amused themselves by trying to write their own. Only Mary Shelley's tale was ever completed, and subsequently became an important contribution to the genres of Gothic horror and science fiction. Baron Frankenstein, 'the pale student of unhallowed arts,' in his *hubris* usurpates the prerogatives of the Creator, by collecting skulls and bones and moldering flesh from churchyards, and putting them together in the shape of a horrendous monster, a blasphemous imitation of the image of the Creator. (For this sin he has been doomed by the cinema to be constantly confused with his monster.) A vital ingredient in the transformation is electricity – for Mary Shelley hardly more than a symbol, a rare word connecting the biological with the metaphysical. The monster, more pitiful than horrible in its hideousness, asks weak-willed Frankenstein for a companion. Revolted by what he has done, Frankenstein refuses, and his creation, endowed with superhuman strength and a fierce thirst for revenge, turns against his creator and the world.

Frankenstein is an attempt to give the Gothic story an air of scientific plausibility; Frankenstein himself is the scientist who oversteps his limits in his search after knowledge, the Faustian man who enquires into things 'man is not meant to know.'

Frankenstein was soon to conquer the other media; as early as July 26, 1823, an adaptation by Richard Brinsley

OCT.

Famous FANTASTIC *Mysteries*

10¢

A POPULAR PUBLICATION

THIRD PERSON SINGULAR
by **CLEMENCE DANE**

THE ISLAND OF DR. MOREAU
A NOVEL OF
SPECTRAL TERROR
by **H. G. WELLS**

Peake was staged in the English Opera House: *Presumption; or the Fate of Frankenstein*, and others followed. By 1826 Frankenstein was in Paris (*Le Monstre et le Magicien*), 1825 in New York; in 1927 there is Peggy Webbling's *Frankenstein* and in 1931 the first film directed by James Whale, followed by about a dozen which made the name of Frankenstein familiar even to those who had never heard the name Shelley.

A later novel in the tradition of black romanticism, and a kind of marginal science fiction, was Robert Louis Stevenson's *The Strange Case of Dr. Jekyll and Mr. Hyde*, written in three days in 1885 after an especially vivid dream. Stevenson (1850–94) burned the manuscript in response to criticism by his wife, who claimed that it lacked allegory, and rewrote it in another three days, but continued to polish it for months afterwards. This fine example of the *doppelgänger* motif made Stevenson's reputation as a writer. The attempt to introduce scientific verisimilitude qualifies this horror story as seminal. A chemical substance wakens 'the brute that slept within me,' turning gentle Dr Jekyll into Mr Hyde, his darker self. 'That child of Hell had nothing human; nothing lived in him but fear and hatred,' and this creature grows stronger, until Dr Jekyll can no longer control the transformation.

Third in this line of moral allegories is the 'theological grotesque,' *The Island of Dr. Moreau* (1896) by H. G. Wells. Just as Frankenstein attempted to create life, and Dr Jekyll experimented with his own nature, Dr Moreau in Wells's story makes grafting experiments with animals, turning them into caricatures of man. Having left England in the wake of anti-vivisection protests, Dr Moreau – like Wells himself a disciple of Thomas Huxley – retreats to his private island, where he can play God to his creatures. Moreau represents the scientist for whom nature is governed by blind chance, and is therefore cruel; unchecked by ethical considerations, he is interested only in the pursuit of pure knowledge. Like Frankenstein, Dr Moreau is finally killed by his creatures, and the inhabitants of the island revert to a wholly animal state.

(*Opposite*) *Cover illustration, by Lawrence, to Wells's* The Island of Dr. Moreau *in* Famous Fantastic Mysteries, *one of the pioneer sf magazines.* (*Bottom*) *Young Victor Frankenstein in the Baron's well-equipped laboratory: a still from the Hammer Films production* The Horror of Frankenstein. (*Below*) *Dr. Jekyll gets a good look at himself as Mr. Hyde in the 1932 production of Stevenson's tale.*

The invasion from Mars

The tables turned: visitors (obviously hostile in the imagination of earthling writers and artists) come to Earth from Outer Space.

On October 30, 1938, at 8 p.m. Eastern Standard Time, the Martians landed in New Jersey. At least that was what thousands of terrified listeners thought who had tuned in to Orson Welles's radio broadcast of H. G. Wells's *The War of the Worlds* (book 1898, serialized in *Pearson's Magazine* from April to November, 1897). The ensuing panic formed the subject of a book-length study by Hadley Cantril (*The Invasion from Mars*, Princeton University Press, 1940). And indeed, the account was frightening enough: 'Good heavens, something's wriggling out of the shadow like a grey snake! Now it's another one, and another! They look like tentacles to me.'

Author H. G. Wells got the idea for his acknowledged classic of interplanetary invasion from a chance remark made by his brother Frank: 'Suppose some beings from another planet were to drop out of the sky suddenly and begin laying about them here!' In the book, the horribly alien Martians, whose motives are quite incomprehensible to man, treat the humans as the Europeans have treated the Tasmanians: as an obsolete race. The Martians are 'intelligences greater than man's and yet as mortal as his own,' minds that are to our mind 'as ours are to the beasts in the jungle, intellects vast, cool and unsympathetic . . .' 'We know now that as human beings busied themselves about their various concerns they were scrutinized and studied, perhaps almost as narrowly as a man with a microscope might scrutinize the transient creatures that swarm and multiply in a drop of water.' The Martian reign of terror, the scenes of destruction, are of an extraordinary vividness, and to the shocked Victorians prophesied what World War I and its aftermath held in store for mankind. For the first time, the horrors of modern warfare were described. Wells's concern – a warning for civilization – is evident from the way he presented the Martians as an advanced race, and how man's 'complacent, confident assumption of the future and his place in the universe' is thoroughly shaken. When the Martian super-beings are finally killed, it is not by some human action but by quite ordinary bacteria, harmless for man, but deadly for the unprepared invaders. In *The War of the Worlds* H. G. Wells established one of the paradigms of the genre; one has only to set it beside Robert A. Heinlein's *The Puppet Masters* (1951) to see how much modern sf owes to Wells – and how much was lost in the transition to the sf magazines; the heat-ray is still here, but the parable has died.

AMAZING STORIES

Stories by
H.G. WELLS

A STREET AND SMITH PUBLICATION

Doc SAVAGE
MAGAZINE

APRIL 1933

10 CENTS

THE LAND OF TERROR
BOOK-LENGTH NOVEL
COMPLETE IN THIS ISSUE

Long before the first sf magazines were born, the fan on the street could buy literally hundreds of cheap novels, all starring a single hero. The most successful of these early sf dime novel series were written by Luis P. Senarens (1865–1939), the 'American Jules Verne,' under the pseudonym of 'Noname.' First published in the paper *Boys of New York*, the adventures of his Frank Reade, Jr, a teenage inventor and the forerunner of Tom Swift, made up 191 volumes of the Frank Reade Library, beginning with 'Frank Reade, Jr, and his New Steam Man; or, the Young Inventor's Trip to the Far West' (September 24, 1892). This series featured many futuristic contraptions, including armored cars, flying vessels, helicopters, electrical submarines and robots.

More clearly characteristic of the sf genre was the German series 'Captain Mors' (*Kapitän Mors, der Luftpirat*), which flourished in weekly installments of 32 pages each from c. 1908 to 1914. Patterned after Verne's Captain Nemo or Robur the Conquerer, Mors is a cosmic Robin Hood, whose exploits are often played out against an interplanetary background, as in the stories 'Deathly Voyage on a Martian Canal,' 'On the Crystal Moon of Saturn,' 'At the Borders of the Solar System,' or 'The Secret of the Meteor.' Captain Mors did his share in fighting primeval monsters on other planets, and in many ways this series anticipated the 'space operas' of later years.

Even today, the one-hero series are not dead, and a few of the old dime novel and pulp heroes have survived in paperback, such as 'Doc Savage' and Edmond Hamilton's 'Captain Future'

(Left and above) Perennial sf heroes, 'Doc Savage' and 'Operator No. 5.' (Overleaf) Captain Mors, a cosmic Robin Hood, whose exploits were serialized in early 20th-century German pulp magazines.

of the 'thirties and 'forties. 'Perry Rhodan' is a current *echt* dime-novel series that enjoys an unprecedented success in Germany, each issue selling hundreds of thousands of copies. Written by a team of German authors, 'Perry Rhodan' is an sf compendium of sorts, with nearly all the sf themes and plots ever devised rolled into one gigantic saga comprising close to 800 issues to date – and no end in sight. Translations in the U.S., the Netherlands, France and Japan testify to the international popularity of these potboilers.

Dime novels and pulp heroes

34 Kapitän Mors im Meteorstein = Regen.

Mit großer Gewalt saußen die Steine um Kapitän Mors gegen die Wände des Weltenfahrzeuges.

Cyrano de Bergerac: journeys to the moon

A modern caricature of Cyrano being launched.

The real Cyrano de Bergerac (1619–55) had little in common with the hero of Rostand's comedy which shaped modern opinion of him. Born in Paris, he was one of the most feared duelists of his day, a 'brave devil' known to draw his sword on the merest glance at his prominent nose. Cyrano died an ignominious death when a log fell on his head; the injury killed him in the prime of his life.

Curiously enough, the same man who forced his way by sword point into the lectures of the philosopher Gassendi, wielded one of the sharpest pens of his time. His two cosmic voyages, *Les Etats et Empires de la Lune* (about 1642) and *Les Etats et Empires du Soleil* (1656), parody previous cosmic voyages and present a mocking mirror of humanity. Just as Cyrano had aroused laughter by expressing the opinion that 'the Moon is a World like ours, to which this of ours serves likewise for a Moon,' the first-person hero of his book is put on trial for heresy on the moon – because he had dared to affirm to the lunarians that the Earth is likewise an inhabited world. Together the two books take up many of the themes of his cosmic predecessors, from Lucian to Kepler and Godwin, and indeed, Cyrano meets no other than Domingo Gonsales on the moon (cf. p. 71).

Cyrano contributed several original devices for reaching the moon. His first attempt was made by means of 'a great many Glasses full of Dew, tied fast about me; upon which the Sun so violently darted his Rays, that the Heat, which attracted them, as it does the thickest Clouds, carried me up so high, that at length I found myself above the middle Region of the Air.' Fearing to shoot past the moon Cyrano began to break his bottles, but broke so many that he fell back to Earth and landed in New France, Canada. Among his later attempts was a first flight by fire-cracker-propelled rocket power.

British rocketry expert Arthur C. Clarke also claims for Cyrano the invention of the ram-jet. This flying machine consisted of a large box with a hole at each end, and built of convex and concave burning-glasses to focus the sunlight in its interior, heating up the air there: 'I foresaw very well, that the vacuity that would happen in the isohedron, by reason of the sunbeams, united by the concave glasses, would, to fill up the space, attract a great abundance of air, whereby my box would be carried up; and that proportionately as I mounted, the rushing wind that should force it through the hole, could not rise to the roof, but that furiously penetrating the machine, it must needs force it upon high.'

In Cyrano's works, 'scientific' means of space travel were liberally mixed with more fantastic ones; in one journey he is drawn to the moon, the fire-crackers having run out by virtue of animal marrow smeared over his body, a substance which is attracted by the moon; and his return is instrumentated by an attendant spirit. Although he was well-versed in the scientific problems of his time, and freely discussed astronomy, mechanics, thermo-dynamics, atomistics, magnetism and physiognomics in his work, natural and supernatural means of space travel were all one to him.

A representation of Francesco Lana's flying machine, another early moon-traveller.

The father of science fiction: Hugo Gernsback

One man is the undisputed founder of modern science fiction: Luxembourg-born Hugo Gernsback (1884–1967). On April 5, 1926, the first periodical in the world devoted exclusively to sf (although the term didn't exist then) appeared on American news-stands: *Amazing Stories*. With *Amazing Stories* science fiction – a term coined by Gernsback himself in 1929 – became a

distinct and separate branch of publishing, and a 'field' of writing. Born on August 16, 1884, Gernsback landed in the U.S. in February 1904, with the invention of a new battery already to his credit. Interested in electricity from the beginning, in 1908 he started *Modern Electrics*, the first radio magazine in the world, wrote the first book on radio broadcasting, *The Wireless Telephone* (1910), and designed the first radio home set. He was eager to expand the boundaries of science, and had absorbed the fantastic work of Wells, Verne and Poe; consequently, when he had to fill some pages in the April 1911 issue of *Modern Electrics*,

he hurriedly wrote the first of twelve monthly installments of *Ralph 124 C 41+*, a science fiction novel. Of no literary merit, the fast-moving story is nevertheless remarkable for the large number of technological prophecies it contains, most of which have come true: weather control, plastics, liquid fertilizers, hydroponics, tape recorders, television, microfilm, a sleep-teaching device, solar energy, space travel, and a good many more. It must be said that many of these devices are already to be found in the work of Kurd Lasswitz, whom Gernsback may have encountered, and the opening scene of *Ralph 124 C 41+* bears an uncanny re-

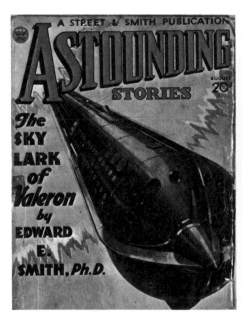

semblance to Albert Robida's *La vie électrique*, which Gernsback may have read either in French or German. Ralph, the hero of this 'Romance of the Year 2660', is one of only ten individuals entitled to carry the plus sign, denoting genius, after his name; and this name itself is a clever pun: 'one to foresee for another'. The plot, which involves the abducting of the heroine by a Martian, and a running battle in space, is typical of what later came to be dubbed – by sf fan and writer Wilson Tucker – as 'space opera'.

In 1923 Hugo Gernsback published a special 'Scientific Fiction Number' of his magazine *Science and Invention*, but it was not until three years later that he took the plunge of putting a magazine on the market that offered nothing but 'scientific fiction' or science fiction. Although the magazine was an immediate success, some legal anomaly forced Gernsback's Experimenter Publishing Co. into bankruptcy in 1929. He immediately started *Science Wonder Stories* and even added a number of other magazines, mostly short-lived, such as *Air Wonder Stories*, *Science Wonder Quarterly* and *Scientific Detective Monthly*. In 1936 he was forced to sell *Science Wonder Stories* to Standard Magazines, who soon retitled it *Thrilling Wonder Stories*, and not until 1953 did he make an attempt to return to sf publishing with *Science Fiction Plus*. But the development of science fiction had bypassed his concept of technological forecasting, which became known as 'Gernsback's delusion', and the magazine folded after seven issues. In 1952 Gernsback was guest of honour at the 1952 World Science Fiction Convention in Chicago, and, beginning with the World Con of 1953, popular works of science fiction were awarded little silver rockets, logically labelled 'Hugos' to honour the 'Barnum of the Space Age' (*Life*, 1963), who invented the term 'science fiction' and, some say, the thing itself.

Cover illustrations to some issues of Hugo Gernsback's several magazines, all of which contributed uniquely to the popularization of sf and the encouragement of its authors and artists.

Tsiolkovsky, the Russian father of rocketry

A page from Tsiolkovsky's manuscript of Free Space. The sketch is of a jet-propelled space ship. The cannon on the right of the ship fires spherical projectiles and its recoil propels the vessel.

The Sun was dazzlingly bright and seemed almost blue. Shielding our eyes with our hands to protect them against the glare of the Sun and the brightness of our surroundings, we could see the stars and planets which were also, for the most part, tinted blue. Neither stars nor planets twinkled, which made them like silver-capped snails studding the black firmament.

(Konstantin Tsiolkovsky, 'On the Moon; A Tale of Fantasy')

Some of the most significant contributions ever made to the field of rocketry came from a schoolteacher in the small Russian provincial towns of Borovsk and Kaluga: Konstantin Tsiolkovsky (1857–1935), the author of a body of truly prophetic science fiction. 'There is nothing that engrosses me more,' he confessed shortly before his death in 1935, 'than the problem of overcoming terrestrial gravity and of making flights into space.' As early as 1878, Tsiolkovsky was sketching fantastic futuristic vehicles and writing of 'free space,' but his work did not find a publisher until 1883. In 1892 the Moscow magazine *Vokrug Sveta* ('Around the World') presented his first sf tale, 'On the Moon,' interesting in its detailed description of surface conditions on the moon and its use of the dream device. Like Kepler, Tsiolkovsky was foremost a scientist, and his science fiction served only as a vehicle for the communication of data; 'On the Moon' may well be a late descendant of Kepler's *Somnium*. In 1895 his *Dreams of the Earth and the Sky and the Effects of Universal Gravitation* promoted the idea of building an artificial Earth satellite for scientific purposes. As a prophet Tsiolkovsky was successful: reaction motors, 'solar motors' (solar cells), space suits, signal communications between planets by light rays, are all to be found in the work of this early Russian pioneer of astronautics and science fiction, who, neglected by the Czarist regime, received high honors after the Socialist Revolution and died a famous scientist.

. . . and two Hungarians

Maurus or Mór Jokai (1825–1904) was given a state burial when he died as Hungary's most popular author, with over a hundred books to his credit.

In 1874 he published *The Novel of the Coming Century* (*A jövö százád regenye*), one of the most remarkable futuristic works of the nineteenth century. This long, colorful novel presents almost anything that can happen in popular fiction, and introduces such fantastic devices as 'ichor,' a glass-like substance that is flexible and unbreakable, ideal material for armor or bullets, which anaesthetize but do not kill. Long before Jules Verne's *Robur the Conqueror* (1886) the hero of Jokai's novel built a flying machine powered by electricity. Nor did Jokai fail to realize the potential of the airship as a weapon; he assumed that its terrible power for destruction would bring about a reform of the world: 'This invention will force the million prepared to destroy each other to disarm, it will return cannon and rifles to the furnaces to cast them into industrial equipment, it will send the soldier home to plough the fields . . .' The most fantastic occurrence in the book is the arrival of a comet in the solar system. This cosmic vagrant destroys the rings of Saturn, threatens to devastate Earth, provides the moon with its own atmosphere, and finally settles down as another planet.

In *Oceania*, another of his several fantasy novels, Jokai chronicled the fall of decadent Atlantis through an earthquake.

Also remarkable is the work of Frigyes Karinthy (1887–1938), whose short stories delve into visions of suspended animation, self-reproducing machines and beings who communicate (as did Godwin's Lunarians) by musical sounds. *Voyage to Faremido* (*Utazás Faremidóba*, 1917), one of Karinthy's two sequels to *Gulliver's Travels*, written before Karel Čapek's *R.U.R.* and before the birth of cybernetics, is a skillful satire, describing the contemptible and imperfect nature of man in comparison to cybernetic machines.

Title-page of the German edition of Mór Jokai's The Novel of the Coming Century.

Mór Jokai.

Title-page of the first edition of The Novel of the Coming Century.

ERB·DOM

To Barsoom! The sf works of Edgar Rice Burroughs

PIT CAPILI 9/70

(*Above*) *Cover of* E(*dgar*)R(*ice*)B(*urroughs*)*dom magazine, No. 45, 1971, which contained* The Moon Maid.

(*Right*) *Illustration by Frank R. Paul for Burroughs's* The Land that Time Forgot (*Amazing, 1927*).

At 35, Chicago-born Edgar Rice Burroughs considered himself an utter failure, having tried his hand at a long string of jobs, including that of clerk, cowboy, gold miner and salesman. Yet the publication of 'Tarzan of the Apes' in the October 1912 issue of *All-Story* magazine made his name overnight as one of the most popular novelists of the century, with eventual translation into some sixty languages. Before 'Tarzan', Burroughs – under the pseudonym of Norman Bean (a printer's typo for 'Normal Bean,' chosen to indicate that the author was quite normal despite the extravagance of his story) – had written one sf novel. *Under the Moons of Mars* appeared as a six-part serial beginning in the February 1912 issue of *All-Story* and was later retitled *A Princess of Mars*. Pursued by Indians, Captain John Carter of Virginia, lying in a cave in Arizona, looks up at Mars, named for the god of war ('for me, the fighting man, it had always held the power of irresistible enchantment'), and his longing transports him in a convenient astral body across the void to the red planet, where he finds himself hatching in a great incubator among a number of Green Martians. There he is attacked by Tars Tarkas, the Jeddak of Thark. The Green Martian himself is 15 feet tall, has four arms, gleaming white tusks and eyes mounted on antennae. Only the lesser gravity of Mars enables John Carter to leap aside and thus save his life. After many hair-raising adventures, Carter is elevated to the position of Warlord of Mars and marries the dazzling Deja Thoris, princess of Helium.

Burroughs followed up *A Princess of Mars* with ten more books: *The Gods of Mars* (1912), *The Warlord of Mars* (1913–14), *Thuva Maid of Mars* (1916), *The Chessmen of Mars* (1922), *The Master Mind of Mars* (1927), *A Fighting Man of Mars* (1930), *Sword of Mars* (1934–35), *Synthetic Men of Mars* (1939), *Llana of Gathol* (1948) and *John Carter of Mars* (published posthumously, 1964).

The author himself, an Army Officer during World War II.

Burroughs's Mars is a dying world of deserts, its air has become so thin that it has to be manufactured by the Red Men of Barsoom (Mars) in the great Atmosphere Factory. The planet is peopled by a number of many-colored races, of which the Red Men, living in Helium, Gathol and Ptarth, are the most civilized; and although they have rifles and airships driven by the mysterious 'Eighth Ray,' they – like all the other war-loving Barsoomians – prefer to fight with swords. Bands of Green Men roam the dead ocean floors; in Okar, Yellow Men hunt the wild Apts and Siths; others are the Black Men, the pirates of Barsoom; the Fair Race of Lothar with their phantom Bowmen; a race of headless humans; the cannibals of U-Gor and many others. Hardly consistent, Burroughs's Barsoom is remarkable more for vivid exotic invention than for depth of description. A storyteller above all, Burroughs whirls the reader through one fantastic adventure after another.

To fully appreciate Burroughs one must become hooked at an early age; for older readers he holds little spell, and his crude style dampens the excitement of his action. Of the Martian series the first three books are the best; Burroughs admirers are more apt to claim two other works as sf classics: *The Land that Time Forgot* (1924), which depicts the discovery of an island in the South Pacific, where prehistoric monsters still survive together with seven species of human beings from different stages of evolutionary development, and *The Moon Maid* (1926). In this novel the Earth is invaded and subjugated by a superior but barbarous race from the interior of a hollow moon, until a new human civilization evolves after centuries in the wilderness to shake off the yoke of the oppressors.

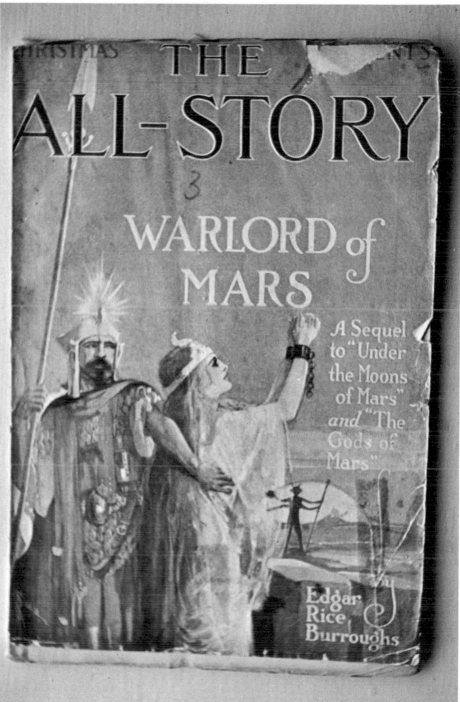

The tales of A. Merritt

Affectionately called 'The Master of Fantasy' by his many fans, Abraham Merritt (1884–1943), an editor for *The American Weekly*, was one of the more successful pulp fantasy authors. Although soundly knocked by some critics for poor plotting, overwriting and stock characters and situations, Merritt's popularity with readers never suffered. Most of his stories follow a standard pattern: a journey into some fantastic realm, the depths of the Earth or some other dimension. His heroes are usually Irishmen or Scandinavians, his villains often Russians or Germans, their nationalities changing to meet the current clichés. The protagonists meet beautiful women with strange-sounding names in the other world (or are lured there by them in the first place). Merritt's stories are full of evil priestesses, frog men, dwarves, the

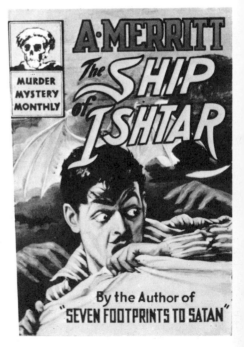

A gallery of illustrations to some of Abraham Merritt's tales of cosmic horror and grotesque fantasy. (Overleaf) The snake Mother in all her cardio-squamous splendor.

half-dead and snake men; and usually there is an additional beauty at the end to reward the hero for his sufferings. Thus in 'The Moon Pool,' first published in *All-Story* on June 22, 1919, and its sequel, 'Conquest of the Moon Pool,' combined in book-form under the former title, the heroes enter an alien land through a mechanism of seven vibrating lights, where a great mystery resides: 'a thing of blinding light, of incredible beauty, and of dark evil beyond the powers of human comprehension,' the Shining One, a pure force. *The Metal Monster* (1920), a less popular sequel, offered the interesting vision of a hive creature, consisting of mobile geometrical units. *The Face in the Abyss* (1923) presented the surrealist image of a giant face weeping tears of molten gold, submerged in a routine cloak-and-dagger action. John Kenton, the hero of *The Ship of Ishtar* (1924), is transported by the antique model of a ship into a fantasy world where he encounters a goddess of dazzling beauty.

Burn, Witch, Burn (1932) was turned into a movie (*The Devil Dolls*) starring Lionel Barrymore in disguise as Madame Mandilip, the sinister old woman who dispatches animated dolls to kill her victims. This novel and the mystery *Seven Footprints to Satan* (1927) are written in a more restrained, effective style. More popular, however, are Merritt's clotted world-pictures with their colorful but imprecise language. Basically, Merritt's stories are unabashed daydreams, which invite the reader to escape into a world ruled by occult powers, evil women and radiant rays, a world conquered by the bold sword-arm.

Fantastic Novels

MAGAZINE

20¢
Now
10¢

Canada 12¢

NOV.

THE
SNAKE
MOTHER
By A. Merritt

Complete
$2.00
Book
Length
Novel

Robots . . .

Karel Čapek's creation, the robot, has become a stock-figure of fantastic literature.

'Bernard Shaw did not write R.U.R. but he probably will. Possibly later on we shall have a variation of R.U.R. by Mr. Shaw and then what we accepted last night as an exceedingly enjoyable and imaginative fantasy will become a dull diatribe. For R.U.R. is Shavian but entertaining. It has force, energy and the sort of fantasy that Barrie has striven unsuccessfully to administer in allopathic doses,' wrote the *New York American* when Karel Čapek's play *R.U.R.* first opened in New York on October 9, 1922.

Following the pattern set by Mary Shelley's *Frankenstein* (1817), Ambrose Bierce's *Moxon's Master* (1908), and the reasoning provided by Samuel Butler's *Erewhon* (anagram for 'nowhere,' 1872), this play, which introduced the word 'robot' (from the Czech *robota*) to the world, enacted in strikingly melodramatic terms the theme of the revolt of the created against their creators. In *Erewhon*, Samuel Butler had brilliantly argued that, by a process of mechanical evolution, machines might develop consciousness, enslave man and finally supersede him. He upheld that man had already allowed himself to become too dependent upon machines, so that, without resort to them, 'the race of man should be left as it were naked upon a desert island, we should become extinct in six weeks.' Therefore the Erewhonians had destroyed all machinery, returned to nature and become a healthy and vigorous breed. In a contrary vein, another Victorian, Edward Bulwer-Lytton, embraced the machine age in *The Coming Race* (1873), postulating a force 'vril' which would liberate man from the drudgery of work.

. . . and golems

Unlike those that appear in sf today, Čapek's robots were what are now called 'androids': artificial humans, mass-produced chemically to do low menial tasks, to be sold as cheap labour, and soon also to be misused for soldiers. At first obedient slaves without a will of their own, the robots quickly acquire emotions and a desire for freedom when one of the chemists alters the formula for their production. Robot emancipation culminates in a robotic revolt, ending with the slaughter of all humans. The emergence of an Adam and an Eve among the initially sexless robots insures the survival of their kind.

Capek's suspenseful masterpiece was written in that venerable city, Prague, which had already seen the creation of another famous artificial being, the golem. Molded from clay, the body of the golem was infused with life by inserting into his mouth a paper with the *shem*, the secret name of God, consisting of 72 letters, written on it. Many Jewish scholars were credited with the creation of golems, ever since the thirteenth century, but the most famous is the one created by the Rabbi Judah Löw (*c.* 1525–1609), called the 'High Rabbi,' who was even acquainted with that strange and moody Hapsburg emperor, Rudolf II, himself interested in the arcane arts. Not exactly a monster, though somewhat sinister and certainly literal-minded to the point of stupidity, this golem was created for the protection of the Jewish community against pogroms, serving as a detective and bodyguard, but when used for profane work, such as doing the laundry for the Rabbi's wife, the golem was likely to get out of control. In some versions of the legend, the golem grows too tall and smothers the Rabbi in collapsing clay when deactivated by having the *shem* pulled out of his mouth.

In Gustav Meyrink's novel *The Golem* (1916), the most famous modern adaption of the legend, the golem does not appear in person but is rather conceived as a symbol for the spirit of the ghetto.

Not created by man, but a product of natural evolution are the strange non-humans called the Newts in Čapek's novel *The War with the Newts* (*Valka smloky*, 1936), but the result is the same: exploited at first, the Newts gain their sovereignty, sink the continents and wipe out the human race. This novel, like Čapek's other works in science fiction, *The Insect Play* (1921), *The Makropoulos Secret* (1923), *Krakatit* (1924, a novel), and *The Absolute at Large* (1927), is a sharp satire on human foibles, yet tempered by warm understanding and a deeply felt humanity.

A still from The Golem.

Space-time jugglers:
E. E. Smith and others

What Jules Verne considered sufficient subject-matter to fill two books – the journey around the moon – is only a preliminary test flight in Edward Elmer Smith's (1890–1965) *The Skylark of Space*, written in 1915–1916 but published in *Amazing Stories*, August-October 1928. Up to that point, sf had been content to travel to the planets of the solar system, as for instance popular astronomer Garrett P. Serviss did to Venus in *A Columbus of Space* (1909), or as Percy Gregg had traveled to Mars in *Across the Zodiac* in 1880. Not so

Illustrations by Marchioni for Jack Williamson's 'Cometeers', by Wesso for 'Galactic Patrol' and by Morey for E. E. Smith's 'Triplanetary.'

E. E. Smith, Ph.D.; as soon as his hero, youthful genius Richard Seaton, discovers the fabulous metal 'X', he builds a space ship, and after a trial run around the moon takes off into interstellar space in his *Skylark*. 'Doc' Smith did what Sam Moskowitz in his flowery language liked to call lifting 'mental horizons to the inspiring wonder of the galaxy.' The flight across 5,000 light years is in chase of a skirt, for Blackie DuQuesne, the diabolically clever and exceedingly pragmatical villain of the *Skylark* novels has ab-

ducted Dorothy, Seaton's sweetheart. After a solid chase the rescue is a matter of course; and in between our heroes manage to get around the universe, visiting strange planets peopled by hideous monsters. Characterized by boyish old-fashioned charm, a series of marvels and dangers, the book had a tremendous effect on pulp sf; and even today its influence is still noticeable in the work of Larry Niven for one, whose heroes feature something of the same naive charm. Smith, in private life a doughnut connoisseur, was in his fiction

a specialist for dreadnoughts; each new book is an escalation, the 'Skylarks' getting bigger all the way, from *Skylark Three* via *Skylark of Valeron* to *Skylark DuQuesne*, written just a few years before the author's death. As in the case of Verne's 'Baltimore Gun Club', it is an escalating playoff between weapons each more invincible than the last.

In his even more popular 'Lensmen' series, Smith describes the conflict between galaxy-wide civilizations, a game of super-cops and super-robbers, with the Arisians representing goodness, and the Eddorians, invaders from another space continuum, absolute evil. Published in magazine form in *Astounding Science Fiction* between 1937 and 1948, the expanded and revised series was ultimately published in six books: *Triplanetary*, *First Lensman*, *Galactic Patrol*, *Grey Lensman*, *Second Stage Lensman* and *Children of the Lens*.

The E. E. Smith escalation pattern was also used by John W. Campbell, Jr in several series: 'Piracy Preferred' (*Amazing Stories*, June 1930), 'Solarite' (*Amazing Stories*, November 1930), 'The Black Star Passes' (*Amazing Stories Quarterly*, Fall 1930), 'Islands of Space' (*Amazing Stories Quarterly*, Spring 1931), and 'Invaders from the Infinite' (*Amazing Stories Quarterly*, Spring–Summer 1932). The formula takes on a grander scale in 'The Mightiest Machine' (*Astounding Stories*, December 1934–April 1935) and 'The Incredible Planet' (1949), where new super-weapons are developed in no time flat, and the author's private physics makes an impressive sleight-of-hand show.

More lightweight are Edmond Hamilton and Jack Williamson. Hamilton ('Crashing Suns,' *Weird Tales* for August–September 1928) shares with Smith the distinction of having opened interstellar distances for sf. Patterned after Dumas's *Three Musketeers*, Williamson's 'The Legion of Space' (*Astounding Stories*, April–October 1934) features a trio of human and likeable heroes, including drinking and complaining Giles Habibula, against whom no lock is safe.

These writers established the 'space opera' patterns that are still popular today, as the many reprints of their novels testify.

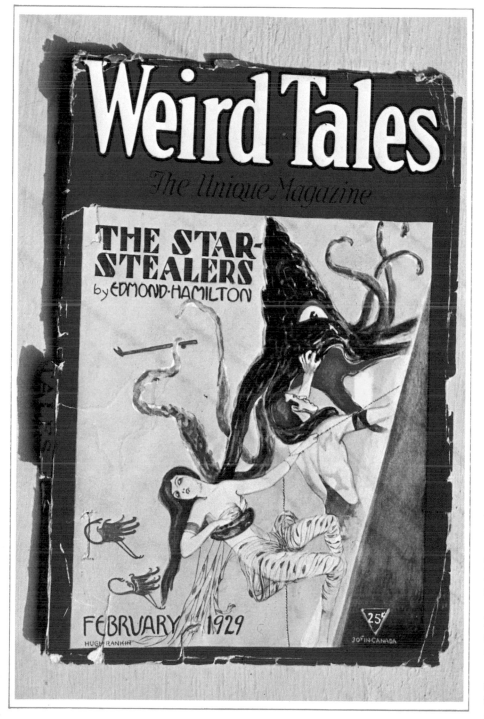

Elder gods and eldritch horror: H. P. Lovecraft

Considered a second Poe by his admirers, H. P. Lovecraft (1890–1937) in fact wrote few stories that could be considered sf proper. Though he was a supreme rationalist-materialist, Lovecraft painted the universe as a place of horror, a warring ground for elder races and gods. Earth offers only a temporary refuge, man is ever in peril, always threatened by cosmic forces from the beyond – sometimes as near as Yuggoth (Pluto), sometimes as far as that 'obscure transgalactic world known in the disturbing and debatable Eltdown Shards as Yith,' and a host of others. 'All my stories', Lovecraft wrote, 'unconnected as they may be, are based on the fundamental lore or legend that this world was inhabited at one time by another race who, in practising black magic, lost their foothold and were expelled, yet live on outside, ever ready to take possession of this earth again.' Over the years he developed a synthetic mythology, the Cthulhu mythos, only partly based on writers such as Poe, Ambrose Bierce, Arthur Machen, Lord Dunsany and

'Of the animals I saw I could write volumes!' – H. P. Lovecraft's fiction was another spawning-ground for new creatures.

Robert W. Chambers. Various other writers helped shape the myth, most of them published in book form by Arkham House, the specialized outfit created by August Derleth solely for the purpose of publishing a selection of Lovecraft's best stories; Arkham authors include Clark Ashton Smith, Robert Bloch, Frank Belknap Lond, Robert E. Howard and Fritz Leiber. They added their own roster of deities and demons to Lovecraft's frightful idiot god Azathoth, 'an amorphous blight of nethermost confusion which blasphemes and bubbles at the center of all infinity,' Yog-Sothoth, Nyarlathotep, Great Cthulhu himself, dwelling in R'lyeh, deep in the sea, and all the rest. Often the reader is referred to fictitious books of heinous lore, the most famous of them being the blasphemous *Necronomicon* or Al Azif of the mad Arab Abdul Alhazred.

In Australia and the Antarctic, at the Mountains of Madness, the huge structures erected by the Great Race who inhabited this world for almost 150,000,000 years, still stand, and Peaslee, the explorer-narrator of *The Shadow Out of Time*, is visited in his dreams by these entities and learns the whole history of the evolution of life on this planet, and of several cosmic races as well. Obviously inspired by Olaf Stapledon's *Last and First Men*, Lovecraft's creation is a splendid vision of the rise and fall of civilizations, a convincing description of alien races. An earlier novel in the same vein, *At the Mountains of Madness*, is somewhat more tedious but exhibits the same sweep of ideas. Another story, 'The Color Out of Space,' is possibly the best sf Lovecraft ever wrote, subtly suggestive in its horror.

ASTOUNDING STORIES

JUNE 1936

CONTENTS COPYRIGHTED 1936

20¢

The Shadow
Out of Time
H. P. Lovecraft

Schachner, Van Lorne,
Coblentz, Corbett, Williamson

The guru of the engineering mind: John W. Campbell, Jr

To a large extent modern sf was shaped by one man who functioned as both author and editor: John W. Campbell, Jr. Only the youngest generation of American sf writers can claim members who are free of any debt to Campbell – those of the older generation have been glad to acknowledge their gratitude for his help. Campbell was born on June 8, 1910 in Newark, New Jersey, had a somewhat difficult childhood, and first became attracted to sf through E. E. Smith's 'Skylark of Space.' While still a student at M.I.T. (and later at Duke University), he contributed super-science stories to the magazines. After his initial success, its peak represented by 'The Mightiest Machine' (*Astounding Stories*, December 1934–April 1936), he turned to writing strangely haunting tales set in the far future, such as 'Twilight' (*Astounding Stories*, November 1934) or 'Cloak of Aesir' (March 1939); these were written under the pseudonym of Don A. Stuart, in order to avoid confusing readers who expected Campbell to continue to emphasize the fantastic gadgetry of super-science rather than delve into subtleties of mood. 'Who Goes There?' (*Astounding Science Fiction*, August 1938), filmed under the title *The Thing*, is one of the most effective horror stories in science fiction to feature the theme of the protean monster. Influential though these stories were, Campbell made his main mark in sf as an editor, and virtually ceased his own writing thereafter. He once explained to Isaac Asimov his reasons for becoming 'only an editor': 'Isaac, when I write, I write only my own stories. As editor, I write the stories that a hundred people write.' Above all, he was a crusader who wanted to influ-

ence others. In editorial after editorial, some of them collected in book form, he expounded his radical views, and some contributors to his magazine deliberately slanted their stories according to the latest wind from the editorial offices. Although Campbell propagated much pseudo-science psionics, Dianetics, the Hieronimus machine or the fabulous 'Dean drive,' and was an authoritarian right-winger, he was personally a kind man and did much, when at the summit of his editorial career, to improve the quality of magazine sf: more so, in fact, than any other man. His death on July 11, 1971 was a severe loss to the world of science fiction.

Created in man's fantasy, the space ship becomes a vehicle by which his imagination may leave Earth. John W. Campbell, Jr, applied his training as an engineer to the fantasy of his science fiction. (Below) Illustrations from the tales he wrote under the pseudonym 'Don A. Stuart.' (Right) A scene from The Thing, *the film version of his 'Who Goes There?'*

The golden age of sf

Until recent years, American science fiction has primarily been a phenomenon of magazine publishing, ever since Hugo Gernsback founded *Amazing Stories* in 1926. Other magazines followed his lead, many of them short-lived. But one of his competitors stands out as the undisputed leader in the field. First published as a space opera magazine under the title *Astounding Stories of Super-Science* in February 1930, the magazine changed its name the following year to *Astounding Stories*, then (in March 1938) to *Astounding Science Fiction*, until finally in February 1960 it became *Analog Fact & Science Fiction*. F. Orlin Tremaine, the magazine's second editor, announced a policy of 'new thought variants' in 1933 but the stories he presented relied heavily on sensation and gimmickry. With the October 1937 issue, Tremaine turned over the editorship to John W. Campbell, Jr, then considered one of the greatest sf writers of the day, and the appointment was to usher in what is now known as the 'Golden Age' of science fiction. Campbell found and encouraged a host of new writers, many of whom are still esteemed today. In addition, some old hands (notably Clifford D. Simak and Jack Williamson) adapted their writing to the modern trend. Between 1939 and the middle of 1943, Campbell published some of the most popular stories ever to appear in sf magazines: 'Slan' by A. E. Van Vogt, 'Microcosmic God' by Theodore Sturgeon, 'Methuselah's Children' by Robert Heinlein, 'Nightfall' by Isaac Asimov, 'Gather Darkness' by Fritz Leiber, and many more.

The Golden Age ended when many of the new writers were called to help in the war effort, among them Heinlein, Asimov, de Camp and Hubbard. *Astounding* continued to lead the field, but the concentration of original new work was never again as high as in those fabled early years. In 1949 and 1950, stiff competition was offered by *The Magazine of Fantasy* (later retitled *The Magazine of Fantasy and Science Fiction*), edited by Anthony Boucher, and *Galaxy*, edited by Horace L. Gold. Both publications helped set new standards of literacy in the genre. Nevertheless, *Astounding/Analog* continued to exercise a powerful influence on sf, despite the idiosyncrasies of its editor; and although it is often called a hobby magazine for retired engineers, it continues to sell more copies than any other sf magazine. After Campbell's death, Ben Bova became its editor.

(Opposite) Illustrations to two early sf stories published in Astounding *and written by L. Ron Hubbard, who was later to found the Church of Scientology.*

Many established writers were first published in pulp magazines. One letter to the editor of Astounding Science Fiction *for April 1939 reads, 'I'm a writer myself – amateur, so far. Give me time, Ray Bradbury.'*

SOLDIER
MOVE
ON

MESSIAH SAY—

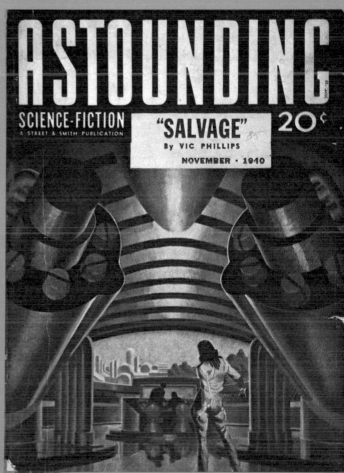

Living suns and sentient planets: Stapledon and Lewis

William Olaf Stapledon stated that he owed the inspiration for his grandiose chronicle of the future, *Last and First Men*, to a vision he once had in Wales, of age of man following upon age of man, each epoch hunting in vain for an ever-elusive happiness. Born in 1886, the British professor of philosophy published his famous novel in 1930. It is a record of the future history of mankind, covering eighteen generations from the present up to the year 2,000,000,000. Following the world empire of the present 'First Man,' a second level of man develops, one gifted with a greater sense of community, but which is attacked by Martians in a series of invasions and ultimately destroyed. After 40 million years, a new species emerges: small in stature, practical-minded, endowed with an extraordinary grasp of music and the graphic arts. Biological control enables this Third Man to remake himself into the Fourth Man, a computer-like brain machine, which in turn creates a new species, Fifth Man. Fifth Man develops a method of time-travel but only into the past. The history of the race continues to reel off until finally Eighteenth Man appears, incorporating the positive features of all previous races to crown the history of Man as the ultimate creation of that spirit which permeates the process of evolution in the universe.

Vast as the developments sketched out in *Last and First Men* may be, they represent only a single episode in *Star Maker* (1937), which attempts to encompass no less than the history of the entire universe. Whereas in *Last and First Men* the role of narrator is taken by the 'last man on Neptune,' in *Star Maker* a contemporary Englishman

Cover design of Stapledon's Odd John, *a Galaxy paperback reprint.*

witnesses the wonders of the cosmos. Echinoderms, neutiloids, arachnoids, ichthyoids – these are a few of the many strange forms that intelligent life has taken in the universe. Immense galactic empires have learned to influence the course of the stars, but the stars are sentient beings and object to being moved by setting off titanic explosions. (A symbiosis between stars and galaxies solves the crisis.) Finally, the various races and cultures merge into a single cosmic consciousness to await the coming of the 'supreme moment' of the cosmos, the appearance of its creator, the Star Maker.

Subsequent generations of authors, with little regard for the mythic beauty, tragic dignity and philosophical splendor of Stapledon's vision, have merely mined it as a quarry for plots and motifs. Two other novels by Stapledon have never been surpassed: *Odd John* (1935), the story of a superman who is simultaneously mankind's victim ('Homo sapiens is a spider trying to crawl out of a basin, the higher he crawls, the steeper the hill. Sooner or later, down he goes. He can make civilization after civilization, but every time, long before he becomes really civilized, skid!'), and *Sirius* (1944), the tragic history of an intelligent dog who has left the brute level of his ancestors, and yet much like man himself has retained many of his animal traits.

Dust jacket of Stapledon's Last and First Men, *the first edition.*

His mind, like so many minds of his generation, was richly furnished with bogies. He had read his H. G. Wells and others. His universe was peopled with horrors such as ancient and medieval mythology could hardly rival. No insect-like, vermiculate or crustacean Abominable, no twitching feelers, rasping wings, slimy coils, curling tentacles, no monstrous union of superhuman intelligence and insatiable cruelty seemed to him anything but likely in an alien.

These are the thoughts of Clive Staples Lewis's (1898–1963) hero Ransom once he has arrived on Mars in a space ship. *Out of the Silent Planet* (1938), 'the most beautiful of all cosmic voyages, and in some ways the most moving' (Marjorie Nicholson in *Voyages to the Moon*), is utterly different from all other space journeys. Not physical action, not just description of the marvelous was the author's aim (although the book itself is more marvelous than many that have gone before and come after it); Lewis actually followed the course he had praised in his essay 'On Stories', speaking of David Lindsay's strange interplanetary journey *A Voyage to Arcturus* (1920): 'He is the first writer to discover what "other planets" are really good for in fiction. No merely physical strangeness or merely spatial distance will realise the idea of otherness which is what we are always trying to grasp in a story about voyaging through Space: you must go into another dimension. To construct plausible and moving "other worlds" you must draw on the only real "other world" we know, that of the spirit.'

For Lewis, space was the 'womb of worlds,' no barren place, and Malacandra (his name for Mars) was an abode for higher beings, the Sorn and Hrossa.

The inhabitants of Malacandra and Perelandra (Venus) are equipped with immortal souls; however, unlike the citizens of more imperfect Thulcandra (Earth) in his controversial trilogy, they have not fallen from grace. Lewis the Anglican attacked 'scientism,' an attitude he thought more common among those professing a scientific attitude than to real scientists. The scientist Weston represents the immoral outlook of the 'opposite side'–including the writers of science fiction; he is

a man obsessed with the idea which is at this moment circulating all over our planet in obscure works of scientifiction, in little Interplanetary Societies and Rocketry Clubs, and between the covers of monstrous magazines, ignored or mocked by the intellectuals, but ready, if ever the

power is put into its hand, to open a new chapter of misery for the universe. It is the idea that humanity, having now sufficiently corrupted the planet where it arose, must at all costs contrive to send itself over a larger area: that the vast astronomical distances which are God's quarantine regulations, must somehow be overcome. This for a start. But beyond this lies the sweet poison of the false infinite – the wild dream that planet after planet, system after system, in the end galaxy after galaxy, can be forced to sustain, everywhere and for ever, the sort of life which is contained in the loins of our own species – a dream begotten by the hatred of death upon the fear of true immortality, fondled in secret by thousands of ignorant men and hundreds who are not so ignorant. The destruction or enslavement of other species in the universe, if such there are, is to these minds a welcome corollary.

Chesley Bonestell's painting of the planet Mars, here used as a cover illustration on Astounding (*December 1954*), *recalls the cosmic voyage tales of C. S. Lewis.*

The French father of science fiction: Jules Verne

(*Below*) *Title-page illustration to one of·the instalments of Verne's* Robur the Conqueror. (*Opposite, above*) *A scene from the Walt Disney film production of* 20,000 Leagues Under the Sea. (*Opposite, right*) *The* Nautilus *sailing among the underwater Rocky Mountains.*

The new works of Jules Verne will be subsequently added to the present editions. . . . Those that already have appeared and those that are yet to appear will in their entirety make up a project which the author took upon himself when he subtitled his work: 'Journeys into the Known and the Unknown.' It is his stated goal to collect all the geographical, geological, physical and astronomical knowledge thus far accumulated by modern science, and to write anew, in the charming manner that is his trademark, the history of the universe.

Thus Jules Verne's publisher P. J. Hetzel introduced the first volume of his edition of *The Adventures of Captain Hatteras*; and Michel Butor, author of a brilliant essay on Verne, claimed for the fictional cartographer of the nineteenth century: 'Very clearly there is a first systematic order in the extraordinary voyages, by the simple fact that Verne aims at a complete description of the world. Their routes

cross over the surface of this globe like a narrow net, with a few inordinately important expeditions into its interior and the vicinity beyond. Did one mark the routes on a map of the world one would see that there are very few real or at that time mysterious realms that haven't been visited by one of his travelers.'

Born February 8, 1828, in Nantes, Jules Verne ran away from home at the age of eleven to become a sailor; soon found and sent home in shame, he vowed, to the subsequent delight of his biographers and readers, that he would henceforth travel only in his imagination – a promise he kept in his more than eighty books, which (according to a report published early in 1972 in *Paris-Match* as the result of a survey conducted by UNESCO) have been translated into some 112 languages (Karl Marx: 133 languages).

After working as a stockbroker and some unsuccessful attempts at the stage, Verne acted on the advice of Hetzel and rewrote a treatise on the exploration of Africa into a story. *Five Weeks in a Balloon* (*Cinq semaines en ballon*, 1863) became an instant hit and resulted in the famous contract with Hetzel that guaranteed the young and inexperienced writer an annual income of 20,000 francs for the next twenty years, for which Verne had to write two novels 'of a new type' per year. The contract was renewed with Hetzel and later with Hetzel's son, and for over forty years Verne's 'voyages extra-ordinaires' appeared in monthly instalments in the *Magasin d'Education et de Récréation*. When Verne finally died on March 24, 1905, the magazine died as well.

Verne's work captured the essence of the nineteenth century, its optimistic spirit, its belief in the bright new vistas opened by science and technology; and it proved that science could be the proper material for fiction. Often considered an author for children – an impression strengthened by his capability for naive wonder – Verne has also been compared to Henri Michaux and André Breton, and was admired by such diverse figures as the Emperor Meiji of Japan, Wilhelm II of Germany, Pope Leo XIII and poet Stéphane Mallarmé.

The silent, demoniac and fanatic man who calls himself 'Nemo' (nobody), that being filled with unrelenting hate for the ships of an unknown nationality, which he sinks by ramming them with his underwater dreadnought, the *Nautilus*, is one of the most enigmatic figures in science fiction. 'I am the law, I am justice,' declares Captain Nemo, who has lost everything: country, wife, children, father and mother. Where oppressors are concerned, the cultured Nemo, owner of a fine art gallery and library, is without mercy; and neither French natural historian Pierre Arronax, nor his faithful servant Conseil, nor the intrepid Canadian harpooner Ned Land, captive guests on the *Nautilus*, ever learn what set the enemy of mankind on his course. (Captain Nemo is later to return in *The Mysterious Island* (*L'Ile mystérieuse*, 1875), where his secret is finally revealed: he is an Indian Rajah, dispossessed by the English.) They can simply watch as he sets course around the world – in Jules Verne's *Twenty Thousand Leagues Under the Sea* (*Vingt mille Lieues sous la Mer*, 1869). Seemingly destined never to leave his ship, the guests hunt in the depths of the world's seas, nearly get stranded in the Torres strait, witness an undersea burial amidst a coral wilderness, cross (via a natural tunnel) the isthmus of Suez before the Canal ever was built, discover sunken Spanish treasure ships, reach the South Pole under the ice, fight with an octopus – and are finally returned to land from the mouth of the maelstrom that apparently finished off the *Nautilus*. *Twenty Thousand Leagues Under the Sea* is one of the great works of science fiction, a guided tour through a world of wonders on a grand scale.

(*Below, left*) *The* Nautilus, *eery and sleek, a creature of neither the land nor the sea, cruises near the ocean floor.* (*Below, right*) *The crew of the* Nautilus *battle the attacking giant squid in the Disney* 20,000 Leagues Under the Sea. (*Above*) *Three illustrations from an early French edition of Verne's masterpiece.*

The mysterious Captain Nemo

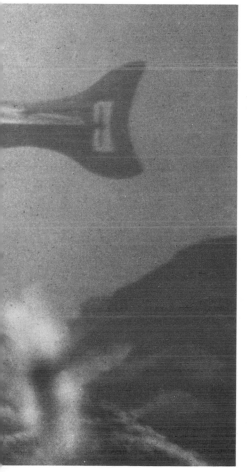

A world in the moon: precursors of sf

The VOYAGE to the WORLD in the MOON.

Printed for John Lover at Little Moorgate next to London Wall near Moorfields.

A world in the moon, and a way to reach it, is one of man's oldest visions. Philolaus, a contemporary of Socrates, thought that the moon was 'inhabited throughout by animals and plants, only larger and more beautiful than ours: for the animals on it are fifteen times stronger than those on the Earth . . . and the day in the Moon is correspondingly longer.' The historian Plutarch wrote *De Facie Orbis Lunare* (*Of the Face in the Moon*), a discussion of the question whether the moon might be inhabitable; if it were another earth yet uninhabited, 'she would have been created in vain and to no end.'

Lucian's Menippus, a Cynic philosopher, fastens the right wing of an eagle and the left wing of a vulture on his shoulders, and sets out to meet Zeus in heaven. As he is resting midway, on the moon, having been spared the fate that befell Icarus, he meets the philosopher Empedocles. In the second of Lucian's moon journeys the author himself is carried with his ship by a violent storm to a region beyond the Straits of Gibraltar that he identifies as the moon. There he witnesses a war between Endymion's moon folk and the solar king Phaethon. In this satire, fantastic battles are staged between Vulture dragoons, Grass riders, Millet shooters, Garlic warriors and Flea archers in one camp, and Ant dragoons, Sky mosquitoes, Sky dancers, Stalk mushrooms, Puppy corns and Cloud centaurs in the other. Lucian was careful to warn his readers that he was writing of 'matters which I neither saw nor suffered, nor heard by report from others; which are in no being, nor possible ever to have a beginning: let no man therefore in any case give any credit to them.'

The next prominent moon voyage was described in the beginning of the sixteenth century, as the courageous knight Astolfo of Ariosto's *Orlando Furioso* (1516) journeyed to the moon in search of Orlando's lost wits – in the very chariot that carried the prophet Elias up to heaven.

Around 1608 the astronomer Kepler (1571–1630) wrote his moon voyage *Somnium*, published posthumously in 1634. While he offered the most scientifically accurate picture of the moon to date – based on the observations made through Galileo's telescope – Kepler employed a dream frame for his story in order to provide a supernatural explanation of the journey: his hero Duracotus is transported to the new world Levania in the moon by a daemon or lunar spirit. This moon is a nightmare world, with lunar nights and days each 15 earth days long; the world is hot and arid by day, and intensely cold at night, when the gigantic, short-lived native creatures of Levania hide in vast subterranean (or sublunar) caves. The influence of Kepler's moon voyage and his antediluvian 'subvolvani' can still be seen in H. G. Wells's *First Men in the Moon* (1901).

Of the early English moon voyages the best is that by Francis Godwin (1562–1633), bishop first of Llandaff, later of Hereford, published in 1638. The Spanish sailor Domingo Gonsales is taken sick and put ashore with his faithful servant Diego on the island of St Helena, where he tames the Gansas, a kind of wild swan, and builds a flying machine. The Spanish ship that rescues him is attacked by English pirates, and later Gonsales escapes from cannibals by means of his flying vehicle. After a series of further adventures the Gansas migrate to the moon, taking Gonsales along with them. 'The ayre in that place I found quiet without any motion of wind, and exceeding temperate, neither hot nor cold . . . Lastly now it is to be remembered that after my departure from the earth, I never felt any appetite of hunger or thirst.' After passing through a region of evil spirits he lands on the moon, a veritable paradise. 'Good groweth every where without Labour, and that of all sort to be desired.' The women there are incredibly beautiful, murder is unknown, vice hated, and the people communicate by means of music. In spite of this, Gonsales eventually takes his leave of the moon and lands in China.

The moon has always held attraction, and not only for lunatics and lovers; other examples of early voyages to our neighbor world are *A Voyage to the Cacklogallinia* (1727) by one 'Captain Samuel Brunt' or Eberhard Christian Kindermann's *Die Geschwinde Reise auf dem Lufft-Schiff nach der obern Welt* (1744).

(*Opposite*) *Domingo Gonsales is rescued from St Helena by the 'Gansas', which fly along pulling his flying machine behind them – a scene from Bishop Godwin's* The Voyage to the World in the Moon. (*Below*) *A modern artist's notion of a moon station.*

Two moon journeys: Verne and Wells

(*Below*) *The ground-crew, alert and tense with attention, await blast-off in Méliès'* A Trip to the Moon, *1902.*

(*Opposite*) *The Union Jack about to be set up on the moon in* The First Men on the Moon (*1964*).

The first attempt to reach the moon by truly scientific means in modern times was made in Jules Verne's novel *From the Earth to the Moon* (*De la Terre à la Lune*), published in 1865. The book contains some descriptions that amazingly parallel twentieth-century actual moon flights. Just like astronauts Frank Borman, James Lovell and William Anders of the historic Apollo 8 flight of 1968, the first men to orbit around the moon, Jules Verne's moon travelers Impey Barbicane, the president of the Gun Club of Baltimore, his adversary

Captain Nicholl and the French journallist Michel Ardan (an anagram for Verne's friend Nadar) took off from Florida, and like the real astronauts they landed on return in the ocean. The elaborate preparations for the moon journey closely resemble the actual start of the rockets of today, although Verne uses, instead of a rocket, a gun 900 feet in length. Drilled vertically into the soil, it is loaded with 400,000 pounds of guncotton which drive a conical projectile into space, at a cost of a mere $5,446,675,000. As Willy Ley has pointed out, in reality the intrepid space travelers' experiences would have been very different from those described by Verne. Verne's space gun would have worked only in a vacuum; on earth, the atmosphere would have acted as an impregnable barrier, and the projectile, despite six billion liters of gas, would have probably been flattened by the atmosphere and would never have left the gun. And the crew, hydraulic shock absorbers and padded capsule notwithstanding, would have been disintegrated into atoms in a few nanoseconds. Despite these flaws, Verne's vehicle of aluminium, with deep-set windows but no air locks, was the first technologically sound space vessel in fiction. Incidentally, Verne was not the first to come up with the idea for a mammoth space gun; as Marjorie Hope Nicholson tells us, in 1728 one Murtagh McDermot published a little book *A Trip to the Moon*, whose hero traveled to the moon by rocket power but returned via gun shot.

Quite different from the almost reportorial account of Verne's story is

the fantasy *The First Men in the Moon* (1901), a poetic description of a dying and stratified society that follows the tradition of older lunar fantasies from Lucian to Kepler. In speaking of this Verne commented on H. G. Wells: 'I make use of physics. He invents. I go to the moon in a cannonball, discharged from a cannon. Here there is no invention. He goes to Mars in an airship, which he constructs of a metal which does away with the law of gravitation . . . Show me this metal. Let him produce it.' (*T. P.'s Weekly*, October 9, 1903). Wells himself, whose scientific training was much more solid than Verne's, was later to admit freely that Cavorite, his anti-gravitational substance, is a fiction that serves merely as one device within a much larger design; in Verne, the journey is everything; in Wells, the point is the goal of the journey, what is found on the moon. His portrait of a truly alien lunar landscape is unsurpassed, and T. S. Eliot called his descriptions of sunrise on the moon 'quite unforgettable.' Lunar vegetation consists mostly of little brown seed pods that open 'eager mouths that drank in the heat and light pouring in a cascade from the newly-risen sun.' The two explorers Cavor and Bedford encounter the Selenites, a race of insect-like creatures, whose society is based on systematic biological conditioning. 'In the moon, every citizen knows his place.' A frightening and grotesque figure is the Grand Lunar: all brain, with a shrunken body and shriveled white insect limbs. 'This quintessential brain looked very much like an opaque, featureless bladder with dim, undulating ghosts of convolutions writhing visibly within . . . shadowy attendants were busy spraying the great brain with a cooling spray, and patting and sustaining it.'

The society of the Selenites is an over-organized order that was increasingly to become the ideal of Wells's later Utopian novels such as *A Modern Utopia* (1905), representing the scientific achievements that go along with such massive specialization; on the other hand it is a warning against the deplorable results of overspecialization, a warning against too much intellectual pride in the achievements of man's intelligence.

(*Left*) *A rocket to the moon, and* (*top*) *the interior: original illustrations for Verne's* From the Earth to the Moon. (*Above*) *The fanciful moonscape from Fritz Lang's* Woman in the Moon (*1929*).

Niels Klim falls to the center of the Earth.

Into the hollow earth

In early fantastic literature the hollow-earth theme was not uncommon. A world of underground caves and tunnels is mentioned in the works of Plato, and was described at length in *Mundus Subterraneus* (1678), a richly illustrated book by Athanasius Kircher, S. J., who was of the opinion that the subterranean realm was inhabited by dragons. In fiction, the idea of worlds in the earth seems to have been used first in Robert Paltock's *The Life and Adventures of Peter Wilkins* (1751). The hero of this tale is the sole survivor of a ship sucked into the interior of the earth near a mysterious island. He discovers a flying race underground, marries one of their women, fathers a number of children, and finally arrives back on the surface.

Of all hollow-earth stories, the most famous as well as artistically the most beautiful is *Nicolai Klimii iter subterraneum* (1741) by Ludvig Baron von Holberg, a Dane. Its hero falls through a cave into the interior of the earth, where he discovers a solar system in miniature, and for a time is a satellite to the little planet Nazar, circling the planet,

(Right) Title-page of the German edition of Niels Klims' Journey Underground *(1828) and four of the wood engravings. (Below) The intra-terrestrial travelers confronted by yet another marvel of astonishment in the film of Verne's* Journey to the Center of the Earth. *(Opposite) Jules Verne discovered the true home of the Loch Ness monster – at the Earth's center – in* Journey to the Center of the Earth.

Niels Klims
Wallfahrt in die Unterwelt.
Bon
Ludwig Holberg.

Aus dem Lateinischen übersetzt
durch
Ernst Gottlob Wolf.

Mit einer Einleitung.

Leipzig:
F. A. Brockhaus.
1 8 2 8.

while a biscuit he had been munching circles around him to demonstrate the laws of motion. He lands on the planet to find himself a symbol of plague in the eyes of the local Nazarite philosophers. After many adventures among strange beings, whose customs are a sharp satire of earthly habits, Niels Klim founds a monarchy, but finally returns to his native country back on the surface of the earth, once again a common man among common men.

Little known, although one of the best novels of its kind, is Giacomo Casanova's *Icosameron, or Edward and Elizabeth* (1788). Edward and his sister Elizabeth are shipwrecked in a maelstrom, but are swept into the interior of the earth in a box of lead. Edward is fourteen, Elizabeth twelve; they marry and beget forty pairs of fraternal twins. During their 324 years' stay (81 years according to our timetable), their descendants increase in number to 600,000 to become masters of this subterranean Eden. Then they return to the light of day, and tell their story to an audience of English lords and ladies.

Journey to the Center of the Earth (*Voyage au centre de la Terre*, 1864) was Jules Verne's contribution to the theme. Following the directions given in an ancient manuscript, a typical German scholar travels via the volcano of Snefell in Iceland into the bowels of the Earth, through epochs of geological time, and to a primeval sea in the center of the earth, where giant ichthyosaurs and plesiosaurs have survived, and a caveman tends a herd of tame mastodons. A stream of lava sweeps the explorers up to the surface.

Several other books are based on the crackpot theory propounded by Captain John Cleve Symmes, that Earth consisted of a series of concentric spheres with holes at the poles. Thus William Bradshaw's *The Goddess of Atvatabar* (1829), John Uri Lloyd's mystical *Etidorhpa* (1895), *The Third World* by Henry Clay Fairman, *The Smoky God, or a Voyage to the Inner World* by Willis George Emerson (1908) and Victor Rousseau's *The Eye of Balamok* (1920). The interior of the Earth is usually peopled by superior people, sometimes remnants of lost Atlantis; or it is a primeval world full of monsters, as in several of Edgar Rice Burroughs's sf novels; in *Tarzan at the Earth's Core* (1930) the 'lord of the jungle' is provided with an opportunity to exchange the familiar African roaming-grounds for the more savage jungles of inner earth.

In Nazi Germany, the *Hohlwelt* theory – that the Earth is not a globe, but a bowl, with the sun inside – was even granted official recognition, as well as incorporated into a number of sf novels; in modern sf, this notion has disappeared.

Isaac Asimov's
three laws of robotics

Isaac Asimov, born on January 2, 1920 in Petrovich, U.S.S.R, and a resident of the United States since 1923, has become a science fiction household name, 'one of America's natural resources' (*Saturday Review*) in the field of science writing. The Good Doctor, as he is affectionately called by his friends, has contributed some of the most persuasive blendings of sf with the mystery story ('The Caves of Steel,' 'The Naked Sun'), has introduced the concept of vast galactic empires peopled wholly by human beings, a sort of latter-day Roman Empire ('Foundation,' 1951; 'Foundation and Empire' 1952; 'Second Foundation,' 1953), and, above all, he has formulated the famous Three Laws of Robotics:

1 A robot may not injure a human being, or, through inaction, allow a human being to come to harm.

2 A robot must obey the orders given it by human beings except where such orders would conflict with the First Law.

3 A robot must protect its own existence as long as such protection does not conflict

with the First or Second Law.

(*Handbook of Robotics*, 56th Edition, 2058 AD)

And yet, beautifully concise and simple as those laws are (and they have since become axiomatic in sf, even in the stories of other writers), persons of lowly rank and dubious mental capabilities have not been ashamed slyly to add another: 'Robots have to behave well at science fiction conventions.'

Dr Asimov's robot stories, collected in *I, Robot* (1950) and *The Rest of the Robots* (1964), follow a fixed, formal pattern; they are detection puzzles, wherein Dr Susan Calvin, robot psychologist who has come to love the iron fellows ('they are clearly a better breed than ourselves'), has to find out the causes behind a seeming violation of the immutable Three Laws, thus restoring order to the world. Of course, the fault never lies with the better iron mankind, but with the fallibility and illogicality of imperfect human beings.

Robots have gone a long way since Frankenstein's unhappy and vengeful monster – in Asimov's stories they are likeable beings like you and me, only more so.

(Opposite) One of Asimov's robots offers hospitality in The Naked Sun. *(Above) Science fiction becomes introverted: the micro-miniaturized travelers through the human body in the film* The Fantastic Journey. *(Below) Asimov's robots make good baby-sitters in* The Naked Sun.

(Overleaf) The UFA film of 1926, Metropolis, *varies the robot theme with a bit of alchemy (the pentangle on the rear wall) and mythology (the robot recalls primitive sculptures of the Great Goddess).*

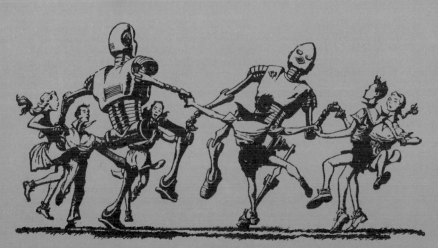

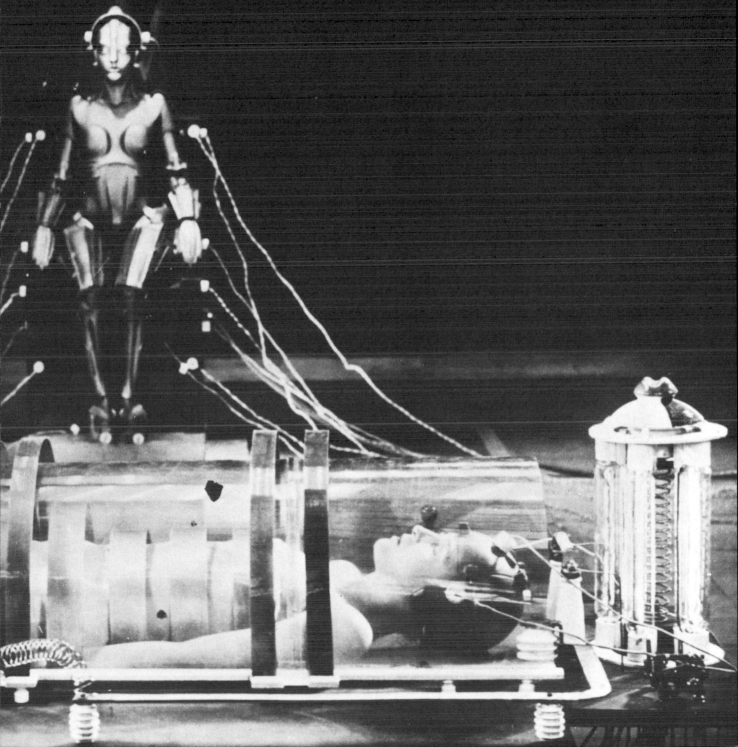

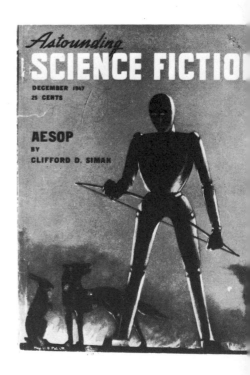

. . . and still more robots

Harry Bates's 'Farewell to the Master' (*Astounding Science Fiction*, October 1940), which was later turned into the film *The Day the Earth Stood Still*, begins with a man arriving on Earth with a gigantic robot, and closes with the portentous line: 'I am the Master,' spoken by the Leviathan, reversing the reader's expectations about who is master and who servant.

Many stories employ the Pygmalion motif, man falling in love with a beautifully wrought machine, as in E. T. A. Hoffman's classic fantasy story,

'The Sandman' (1817). This provided the motif for one of the earliest and still one of the best robot novels, Villier de l'Isle-Adam's *L'Eve Futur* (1886), in which the famous inventor Thomas Alva Edison (who caught the fancy of his time as no other inventor did, appearing as a character in many a sf story) builds a robot in the likeness of a woman who is as beautiful as she is stupid. A British lord becomes so enamored of her charms that he prefers the machine to the real woman. Sentimentalized, the theme recurs in certain

sf stories of more recent vintage, such as 'Helen O'Loy' (*Astounding Science Fiction*, December 1938) by Lester del Rey.

In Clifford D. Simak's famous 'City' series (published in book form in 1952), the robots are faithful servants, duly taking care of the few humans in a world peopled by intelligent dogs, after humanity has emigrated to Jupiter. In still other stories, obedience to man has been so deeply ingrained in the machines that little lost robots wander about in search of a purpose or in

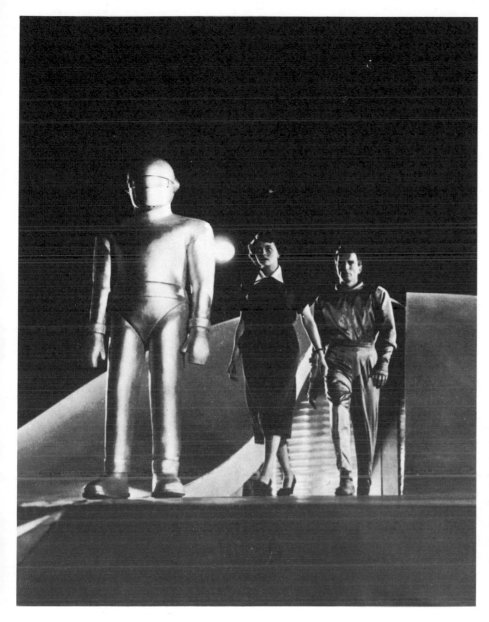

execution of tasks that no longer have any purpose, when mankind has disappeared in the wake of an atomic holocaust.

Henry Kuttner, one of the most versatile writers of the 'forties, produced a series of stories collected as *Robots Have No Tails* (1952), in which he has some good-natured fun with a slightly mad robot who doesn't behave as a good robot should.

No sentimental flattery to man's indispensibility for the beings created by him is apparent in Stanisław Lem's hilarious *Fables for Robots* (1964) and *The Cyberiad* (1965). In the myths and legends of Lem's robots, who have escaped from the yoke of man into the galaxy, man is not presented as the benefactor or even God of robotkind, but as a cruel monster and tyrant, the ultimate horror, pale, weak, flabby, disgusting, a being whose very looks can cause a robot to rust. This cycle of stories extols the creativity and independence of the cybernetic breed, foremost as personified in Trurl and Klapaucius, two friendly robot rivals, who create machines to serve any purpose and out-invent their enemies. Trurl and Klapaucius are the two most wittily elegant knights of a robothood that has emphatically asserted its inborn right to freedom and independence.

Lost worlds:
Arthur Conan Doyle

It will come as a surprise to many that Arthur Conan Doyle's favorite creation was not Sherlock Holmes, the detective who made his name immortal; dearer to Doyle's heart was good-humored and sincere Professor Challenger of *The Lost World* (1912), *The Poison Belt* (1913) and their sequels. Doyle (1859–1930) even used to masquerade as Professor Challenger to amuse his friends, although his contribution to sf is in no way to be compared to the lasting impetus he gave the detective story. The sf counterpart of Sherlock Holmes, Challenger is always busy uncovering some scientific mystery. In *The Lost World*, a novel in the sub-genre of the 'lost race' tales in which H. Rider Haggard (*She*, *King Solomon's Mines*) excelled, Challenger tries to persuade his colleagues that a plateau inhabited by prehistoric monsters exists somewhere in South America and in the face of ridicule sets out to prove his hypothesis. The party ultimately finds a world of strange beasts from the Earth's past, as well as a race of contemporary natives in great need of help. For proof, Challenger takes back

THE STRAND MAGAZINE

Vol. xlii. APRIL, 1912. No. 256.

THE LOST WORLD.

Being an account of the recent amazing adventures of Professor George E. Challenger, Lord John Roxton, Professor Summerlee. and Mr. E. D. Malone of the "Daily Gazette."

BY

ARTHUR CONAN DOYLE.

Illustrated by

Harry Rountree and the late Maple White.

I have wrought my simple plan
If I give one hour of joy
To the boy who's half a man,
Or the man who's half a boy.

FOREWORD.—Mr. E. D. Malone desires to state that both the injunction for restraint and the libel action have been withdrawn unreservedly by Professor G. E. Challenger, who, being satisfied that no criticism or comment in this book is meant in an offensive spirit, has guaranteed that he will place no impediment to its publication and circulation. Mr. E. D. Malone would wish also to express his gratitude to Mr. Patrick L. Forbes, of Rosslyn Hill, Hampstead, for the skill and sympathy with which he has worked up the sketches which were brought from South America, and also to Mr. W. Ransford, of Elm Row, Hampstead, for his valuable expert help in dealing with the photographs.— Streatham, 1912.

CHAPTER I.
"THERE ARE HEROISMS ALL ROUND US."

R. HUNGERTON, her father, really was the most tactless person upon earth—a fluffy, feathery, untidy cockatoo of a man, perfectly good-natured, but absolutely centred upon his own silly self. If anything could have driven me from Gladys, it would have been the thought of such a father-in-law. I am convinced that he really believed in his heart that I came round to the Chestnuts three days a week for the pleasure of his company, and very especially to hear his views upon bimetallism—a subject upon which he was by way of being an authority.

For an hour or more that evening I listened to his monotonous chirrup about bad money

Vol. xliii.—25.

THE STRAND MAGAZINE

Vol. xlv. MARCH, 1913. No. 267.

THE POISON BELT.

By A. CONAN DOYLE.

Illustrated by Harry Rountree.

Being an account of another amazing adventure of Professor George E. Challenger, Lord John Roxton, Professor Summerlee, and Mr. E. D. Malone, the discoverers of "The Lost World."

CHAPTER I.
"THE BLURRING OF THE LINES."

T is imperative that now at once, while these stupendous events are still clear in my mind, I should set them down with that exactness of detail which time may blur. But even as I do so, I am overwhelmed by the wonder of the fact that it should be our little group of the "Lost World"—Professor Challenger, Professor Summerlee, Lord John Roxton, and myself—who have passed through this amazing experience.

When, some years ago, I chronicled in the

Vol. xlv.—25.

Daily Gazette our epoch-making journey in South America, I little thought that it should ever fall to my lot to tell an even stranger personal experience, one which is unique in all human annals, and must stand out in the records of history as a great peak among the humble foothills which surround it. The event itself will always be marvellous, but the circumstances that we four were together at the time of this extraordinary episode came about in a most natural and, indeed, inevitable fashion. I will explain the events which led up to it as shortly and as clearly as I can, though I am well aware that the fuller the detail upon such a subject the more welcome it will be to the reader.

"CHALLENGER FELL, AND AS I STOOPED TO PICK HIM UP I WAS AGAIN STRUCK FROM BEHIND AND DROPPED ON THE TOP OF HIM."

Lord Roxton held up his hand as a signal for us to stop, and he made his way swiftly, stooping and running, to the line of rocks. We saw him peep over them and give a gesture of amazement. Then he stood staring as if forgetting us, so utterly entranced was he by what he saw. Finally he waved us to come on, holding up his hand as a signal for caution.

---

at the little birds under the trees!"

We drew four chairs up to the long, low window, the lady still resting with closed eyes upon the settee. I remember that the monstrous and grotesque idea crossed my mind—the illusion may have been heightened by the heavy stuffiness of the air which we were breathing—that we were in four front seats of the stalls at the last act of the drama of the world.

"THE CHAUFFEUR DOWN IN THE YARD HAD MADE HIS LAST JOURNEY."

(To be continued.)

Conan Doyle's sf novels gave him the opportunity to investigate not the mysteries of human crime and evil, but the possibilities of Nature in a mood of fantastic creation. In The Lost World (*the stills here are from the 1961 and 1925 film productions*), *Conan Doyle's travellers encounter prehistoric monsters on a South American plateau.*

with him a small pterodactyl, which he releases in a lecture-hall; it is last seen flying across the face of the moon.

Even more fantastic is *The Poison Belt* (1913); when the Earth's atmosphere is poisoned by something in outer space, among the only survivors are Challenger and a few friends who camp out in an airtight room in his house. In *When the World Screamed* (1929), Challenger discovers that our planet is a living organism, for when he drills a shaft deep into the Earth's crust, a truly earth-shaking scream issues forth, from none other than Mother Earth herself, a living creature.

Other titles in the series included the weaker novels *The Disintegration Machine* (1929) and *The Land of Mist* (1927), in which Challenger is contacted from the spirit world by his dead wife and converted to spiritualism. Doyle wrote a number of other sf stories, such as *The Horror of the Heights* (*Everybody's Magazine*, December 1913).

In a prophetic novelette *Danger!*, published in *The Strand*, February 1914, Doyle described in detail the dangers of submarine warfare for Great Britain. He was later accused by some readers of having drawn Germany's attention to his country's weakness.

(*Opposite*) The Poison Belt *and* When the World Screamed *are both fantasies of Nature's and Earth's revenge for man's interference.*

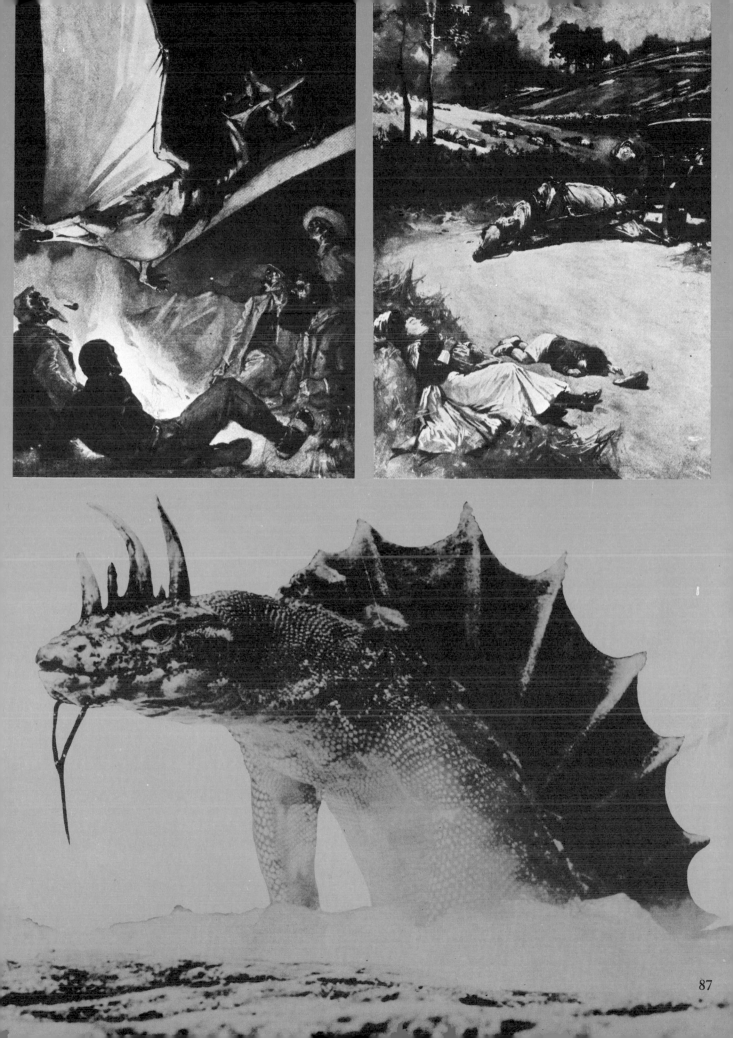

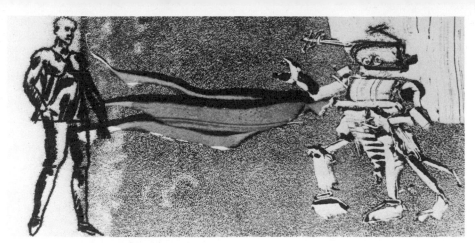

BLACK DESTROYER by A. E. Van Vogt

In A. E. van Vogt's 'Vault of the Beast', a space-monster has the unhappy talent (for itself and its victims) of becoming whatever it touches. In his 'The Monster' (an illustration above from its Hungarian translation) and 'Black Destroyer', evil is defeated philosophically, with the cold truth rather than the scorch of a ray-gun.

'Fans are Slans!' – this is one of the many slogans sf readers invented in response to their favorite reading matter. 'Slan', of course, was the word concocted by Canadian-born (April 26, 1912) Alfred Elton van Vogt for *homo superior*, the race to follow after man. *Slan* became instantly popular when it was published in *Astounding Science Fiction*, September-December 1940. It tells the story of nine-year-old Jommy Cross, a telepathetic orphan of mental and physical superiority. The 'slans' are a hated minority, hunted down and killed by normal human beings. Though not as profound in its treatment of the superman theme as its predecessors, *The Hampdenshire Wonder* (1911) by J. D. Beresford, *Gladiator* (1930) by Philip Wylie, or *Odd John* (1935) by Olaf Stapledon, the book is a fine example of pulp adventure, a fast-paced series of cliffhanger situations.

Van Vogt made his debut in sf with 'Black Destroyer' (*Astounding Science Fiction*, July 1939), an interesting monster story inspired by John W. Campbell, Jr's 'Who Goes There?'; it was the first of a series eventually rewritten into the book *The Voyage of the Space Beagle* (1950), thinly strung together through the character of a scientist-hero whose fictional super-system is called 'nexialism.' Van Vogt's dream of the infallible scientific method emerged most clearly with *The World of Null-A* (1945), a confusing novel featuring a mutant with a dual mind who has many of the attributes of a god-head. During a power struggle of galactic dimensions he is killed several times, only to come back to life again and again. While it purports to be based on *Science and Sanity* by the Polish count Alfred Korzybski, the novel seems to do little more than quote from Korzybski in catchy chapter headings and epigraphs such as 'The map isn't the country.' Despite a merciless dissection by American sf critic Damon Knight, the book became a best seller in France, where it was translated by Boris Vian.

Van Vogt's early work has some deep, irrational appeal that has never been sufficiently explained. Van Vogt himself has described several incidents from his youth that affected him profoundly, such as a severe beating: 'It was so unfair, so completely at variance with the moral teachings I had received, that I was devastated by the defeat.' Beneath the surface play of pragmatism, power and super-forces, his work shows a deep concern with morality. Van Vogt is the tragic case of a writer at odds with himself, a man with an honest desire for truth, but who has consistently fallen victim to the infallible 'techniques' of some pseudo-science: Korzybski's 'General Semantics', Hubbard's Dianetics and Scientology, or the eye-training method of W. H. Bates, all of which have been worked into the fabric of his fiction, together with his own ultra-'logical' systems. In addition, almost all his heroes are supermen whose secret powers are often unknown even to themselves. Van Vogt's novels are often confounded by a kitchen sink full of ideas, and far more solid are his short stories such as 'The Monster' (1948), 'Far Centaurus' (1944) or 'Enchanted Village' (1950). Parts of *The Voyage of the Space Beagle* (1950) or *The Mixed Men* (1952) convey in lyrical passages a true impression of cosmic feeling and human destiny.

Big Brother is watching you: anti-utopia

The focal theme of anti-utopia in science fiction signals a bitter farewell to the vision of a golden age and a perfect society: it is utopia in reverse, *dystopia* (as it is often called), a negative blueprint of the future and an expression of the anxieties of our age. The First World War shattered the hope that things would continually keep getting better, that technology automatically meant progress. Yet the roots of dystopian disillusionment go back to much earlier times, and perhaps the concept of dystopia is the inevitable dialectical corrective to utopia – besides being so much more exciting dramatically than the best of all possible worlds. The development in sf can be clearly ascertained in H. G. Wells, with his ambivalent attitude toward science and society; much of his early work (*The Time Machine*) is quite un-Wellsian, if 'Wellsian,' as his opponents claimed, refers to an attitude of unlimited faith in progress brought about by science and technology. In *The War of the Worlds*, Wells questioned man's supreme role in the universe – as did E. M. Forster in 'The Machine Stops' (1909), which derived its ideas from Wells, but turned them inside out. A future mankind living in hexagonal cells underground is cared for by the machine, isolated from nature and cut off from his roots. When the machine breaks down, mankind dies as well, except for a few survivors who have adapted to life on the surface of the earth.

Most influential on later anti-utopias was Evgeny Zamyatin's *We* (*My*, 1922), a poetical novel written by a member of the Soviet Communist Party whom Stalin later allowed to emigrate to Paris. Never published in the U.S.S.R., *We* is an attack not so much against communism as on its Stalinist perversion; it is a revolutionary work by a man who considered himself a better revolutionary than the men who profited from a revolution choked by terror and bureaucratization. Engineer D-503, the constructor of the space ship *Integral*, falls in love with I-330, a leader of the underground. The state of *We* is a giant city enclosed by a green wall, and ruled by a Benefactor, in which life is regimented down to when and whom one may love. *We* profoundly influenced George Orwell's *1984* (1949), an anti-totalitarian novel communicating an atmosphere of utter despair. Here the world is divided into three power blocs constantly at war with each other in changing coalitions. Orwell's Benefactor is called 'Big Brother,' a figure who may or may not exist. Everyone is spied upon, children are encouraged to denounce their parents, TV allows 'Thought Police' to watch citizens in their homes. History is rewritten to suit the policies of the moment, a synthetic jargon of 'newspeak' perverts the old meanings of words, glaringly obvious in the slogans of the party: 'Ignorance is Strength,' 'War is Peace,' 'Freedom is Slavery.' An unimportant party member, Winston Smith, comes into contact with the underground, tempted by a woman; he experiences a short spell of bliss, but is found out, brainwashed and mercilessly crushed by the system – after he has recognized the error of his ways and learned lovingly to embrace Big Brother.

The third classic anti-utopia, Aldous

Huxley's *Brave New World* (1932), is a humanist's attack on a hedonist Eden, where men are bred in test tubes, conditioned for happiness and engineered for their future roles in society. A passionate plea for human autonomy, even the right to unhappiness, Huxley's novel is prefaced by a quotation from Nicholas Berdyaev, who feared that utopias are realizable. 'But it is possible that a new age is already beginning, in which cultured and intelligent people will dream of ways to avoid ideal states and to get back to a society that is less "perfect" and more free.'

Few of the many anti-utopias after those by Zamyatin, Huxley and Orwell have been as powerful. Huxley himself wrote in *Ape and Essence* (1949) a more horrifying, but artistically inferior novel of a world devastated by atomic war; in German literature, Walter Jens's *Nein, die Welt der Angeklagten* (1950), while echoing its predecessors, achieves some moments of chilling horror; and Anthony Burgess, in *A Clockwork Orange* (1962), presents a future England terrorized by teenage hoodlums.

(*Below*) *A scene from Stanley Kubrick's anti-utopian film* A Clockwork Orange. (*Right*) *One of the Big Brother's anti-sex vigilantes looks as though she is not very happy in her work* (*from the film of* 1984).

BIG BROTHER
IS WATCHING YOU

The illustrator of worlds to come: Albert Robida

Albert Robida's fantastic anticipations ranged from an air-terminal and a restaurant atop one of the towers of Notre-Dame to luxury cruises aboard submarines (see also overleaf).

The first great artist and illustrator who was to apply his talents predominantly to science fiction, and thereby succeed in creating a really anticipatory art, an art that is much more remarkable than most of the written manifestations of the form of his or any other time, was undoubtedly the great Albert Robida (1848–1926). Little known these days even in his native France, he once enjoyed an enviable reputation in his own country, and had many foreign editions in Italy, Germany, Russia and Hungary. His extraordinary illustra-

93

tions and drawings combine a sardonic and sarcastic humor, a feeling for sharp detail, and an uncanny ability to predict the bleaker developments of fashion in the future. Robida was much more than simply an illustrator, putting into pictures what others might have thought of; his imagination was truly of the future. Above all, his work is a delightfully quaint product of the gaslight age–modernity clothed in old-fashioned charm, nineteenth-century vintage pieces pointing to a grim twentieth century.

Robida was editor-in-chief of the humorous paper *La Caricature* (from 1883), in which appeared what is probably his best-known work, *La guerre au vingtième siècle* (*The War of the Twentieth Century*). Robida's startling anticipations include aerial and submarine, chemical and bacteriological warfare, television, radio-directed artillery, and the computer: a robotic French president who signs everything when the proper keys are inserted. Robida started his career by writing and illustrating an amusing parody of Jules Verne, *Voyages très extraordinaires de Saturnin Farandoul dans les 5 ou 6 parties du monde et dans tous les pays connus et même inconnus de Monsieur Jules Verne* (1879). Among his more memorable works are *Le vingtième siècle, roman d'une Parisienne d'après-demain* (1882), *La vie électrique* (serialized in the popular magazine *La science illustrée*) and *L'ingénieur Von Satanas* (1919). Robida illustrated not only his own works, which are more remarkable for their illustrations than their often banal prose and trite plots, but also the 'Baron Münchhausen' tales and books by Rabelais, Cyrano de Bergerac and Swift, among others.

Verisimilitude in science fiction: Edgar Allan Poe

As well as being one of the 'fathers' of the detective story, Edgar Allan Poe (1809–49) is also at least one of the founding fathers of science fiction. In Europe especially he is counted among the originators of the genre; Verne, for instance, gladly acknowledged his debt to him, and indeed used freely many of Poe's ideas in his own stories, such as the denouement of *Around The World in Eighty Days*, taken from Poe's 'Week with Sundays'; with Poe he shared the enthusiasm for logograms, in *The Ice Sphinx* (1897) he even attempted a sequel to Poe's *Arthur Gordon Pym*, and *Five Weeks in a Balloon* shows strong similarities with Poe's 'The Balloon Hoax.'

In his article, 'Edgar Allan Poe – Science-Fiction Pioneer,' Olney Clarke wrote in *The Georgia Review* (1958): 'Poe's role in the creation of the modern science-fiction genre was of primary importance. He was the first writer of science-centered fiction to base his stories firmly on a rational kind of extrapolation, avoiding the supernatural.'

And sf historian Sam Moskowitz notes in *Explorers of the Infinite* (1963):

Basically, Poe's science fiction stories can be divided into two major categories. The first, including such tales as 'MS Found in a Bottle,' 'A Descent into the Maelstrom,' and 'A Tale of the Ragged Mountains,' comprises artistic science fiction in which the mood or effect is primary and the scientific rationality serves merely to strengthen the aesthetic aspect.

In the other group, examples of which are 'Mellonta Tauta,' 'Hans Pfaall,' 'A Tale,' and 'The Thousand-and-Second Tale of Scheherazade,' the idea was paramount and the style was modulated to provide an atmospheric background which would remain unobtrusive, and not take the spotlight from the scientific concept.

In 'The Unparalleled Adventure of One Hans Pfaall' Poe contributed little to the theme of space travel that had not appeared in earlier stories, but established the pattern that is typical of a good deal of sf even today: scientific verisimilitude in some peripheral aspects, along with blatantly fantastic occurrences in others – such as Poe's two-feet tall Lunarians on a world already known to be uninhabitable. In defense of his own story, Poe wrote (not quite accurately) of prior voyages to the moon: 'In these various brochures, the aim is always satirical, the theme being a description of Lunarian customs as compared to ours. In none is there any effort of plausibility in the details of the voyage itself. The writers seem in each instance to be utterly uninformed in respect to astronomy. In Hans Pfaall the design is original, in as much as regards an attempt at verisimilitude, in the application of scientific principles (so far as the whimsical nature of the subject would permit) to the actual passage between the Earth and the Moon.'

The work of Robert A. Heinlein

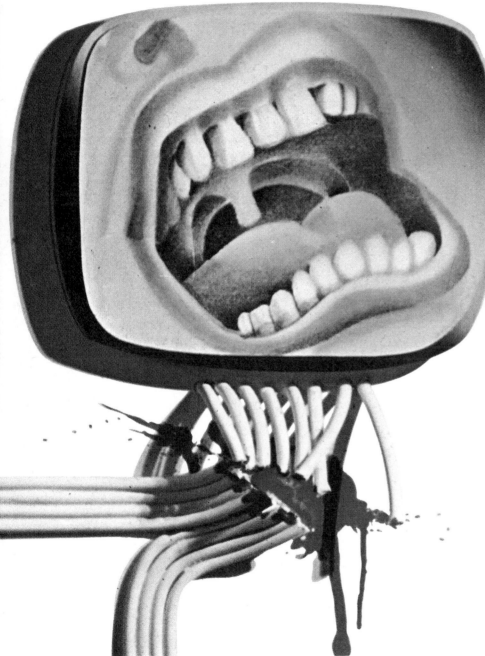

Robert Heinlein's fantastic creations are masterpieces of engineering principles applied to the sf author's creative imagination.

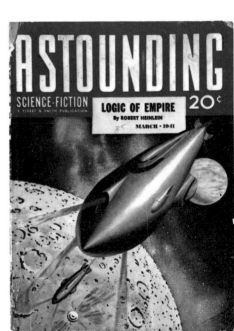

Probably no other sf writer in America today enjoys more popularity than Robert A. Heinlein, born July 7, 1907 in Butler, Missouri. For over thirty years he has been considered one of the prime movers of science fiction. A graduate of the U.S. Naval Academy at Annapolis, he was retired in 1934 because of ill health. Although he was never in combat action, his military experience shaped much of his outlook, and soldiers figure prominently in his fiction as beings of superior wisdom (*Starship Troopers* endorses an ultra-militaristic philosophy). After working in a number of wide-ranging fields, including politics, real estate, mining and architecture, Heinlein tried his hand at sf, having been an avid reader since the dime-novel *Frank Reade Weekly* of his childhood. A first story, 'Life Line,' appeared in *Astounding Science Fiction* in August 1939, and Heinlein soon proved to be one of the most decisive influences in the formation of the 'new' sf of the 'forties as shaped under the editorial guidance of John W. Campbell, Jr. Many current sf writers have learned from Heinlein, who introduced an air of everyday realism: his heroes are no gaping tourists in a world of marvels, but men who take their world of the future for granted. Heinlein's broad background is reflected in his gift for meticulous detail. Yet underlying the realistic presentation is a current of romanticism, and despite the suggestion of everyday life, his heroes are as equipped with talents as other sf characters, hard-headed competent profcssionals (scientists, politicians, engineers, soldiers, busi-

nessmen) who personify an ethic of success. For Heinlein, man is the most dangerous animal alive, to be crossed by others only at their own peril; and his stories are an endorsement of social Darwinism.

Many of Heinlein's works fall under a common plan, his 'Future History' comprising the years from 1940 to 2140; a chart indicating the titles of published and future stories was printed in *Astounding Science Fiction* in May 1941. (This device has since been adopted by other sf writers, including Isaac Asimov, Poul Anderson and James Blish.) Stories that fell outside the pattern were originally published under such pseudonyms as 'Anson McDonald.'

Aside from contributing his new approach to science fiction, the early Heinlein enriched the field with new topics. In 'If This Goes On . . .' he described a successful revolt against a tyrannic theocracy of the future; in 'Universe' he presented the generation-long voyage to the stars, with the space ship forming a closed micro-universe, whose inhabitants have forgotten their origins and purpose (Harry Harrison, Clifford D. Simak, E. C. Tubb, Brian W. Aldiss and others have followed his lead in this type of story); and 'By His Bootstraps' (1941) tied time into a perplexing knot of paradoxes, since then perhaps surpassed in the author's own 'All You Zombies' (1959), an experiment in auto-creation.

After the war Heinlein wrote a series of twelve successful juveniles, among them some of his best works (*Red Planet*, 1949; *Farmer in the Sky*, 1950; *Starman Jones*, 1953), went on to win four Hugos for the best sf novel of the year, and wrote a paperback bestseller in *Stranger in a Strange Land* (1961), a novel of diffuse mysticism that became 'the hippie's Bible' which – as Heinlein's critics are quick to point out – is said to have 'inspired' the drug commune leader and murderer Charles Manson.

In Heinlein's 'Life-Line', Dr Hugo Pinero, 'bio-consultant', uses his 'chronovitameter' to determine the day of a man's death – including his own. Like many sf authors, Heinlein uses a moon journey as a plot – a still from the film Destination Moon.

Time (*Torpeda czasu*, 1923) which
prefigures many of the time-travel
paradoxes of later science fiction.
Slonimski's heroes return to the past
to avert the horrors of the Napoleonic
wars; they succeed in their purpose,
but reap another form of misery in the
end: a classic sf twist.

A Pole on the moon

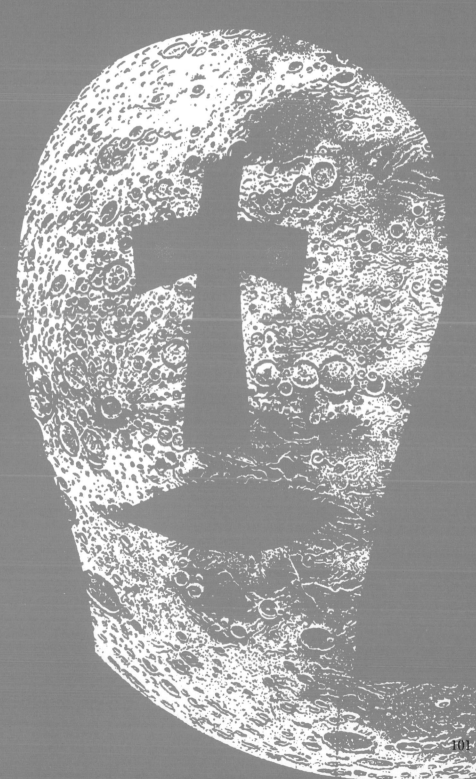

Many European works of science fiction
might have exerted more influence on
the development of the genre, had they
been accessible in English or French.
One such work is the lunar trilogy
written by the Pole Jerzy Żuławski.
Born in 1874 in southern Poland (then
part of the Austro-Hungarian monarchy), Żuławski studied philosophy
in Switzerland, where he obtained a
doctor's degree for a thesis on Spinoza.
A poet, critic, essayist and playwright,
he is best known for *Eros and Psyche*, a
fantastic play inspired by Apuleius.
His lunar trilogy, beginning with *The
Silver Globe* (*Na srebnym globie*, 1903),
can be read even today, and was in fact
translated in the Soviet Union a few
years ago. *The Silver Globe* is the account of a first journey to the moon,
where an expedition discovers a moon
population on the far side. The book
was one of the first in sf to deal with the
theme of religion, for the moon explorers, unable to return to Earth, soon
develop a doctrine to explain their
'exodus.' In the second volume *The
Victor* (*Zwyciezca*, 1910), a single man
flies to the moon 150 years later, without
any knowledge of his predecessors'
fate. There he is welcomed as the
Savior, who is to lead the lunar humans
out of bondage to a species of hideous
monsters. Still other Lunarians hold
that the scriptures are a lie, and that
humans are living in sublunar cities on
the other side of the moon. These
unbelievers steal the space ship of the
terrestrial visitor, who dies a martyr's
death at the hands of the ruling human
class. The trilogy is concluded with
The Old Earth (*Stara Ziemia*, 1911).

Another remarkable Polish sf classic
is Antoni Slonimski's *The Torpedo of*

Ray Bradbury
and the
lost voice
of childhood

For the general reading public, as distinct from avowed sf aficionados, one name stands for science fiction more than that of any other writer: Ray Bradbury, born August 22, 1920, in Waukegan, Illinois. Although he began writing in the lowest pulp magazines, his career skyrocketed within a few years, and he cracked all the important American short story markets, including both Martha Foley's *Best American Short Stories* and the *O. Henry Memorial Award Stories*. Bradbury's first stories of note were horror fantasies for the magazine *Weird Tales*. The best of them were collected in his first book, *Dark Carnival* (New York, 1948), today a coveted collector's item. His first great sf work was *The Martian Chronicles*, published in 1950. A loosely connected collection of short stories, containing gems such as 'The Million Year Picnic,' 'And the Moon Be Still As Bright' and 'There Will Come Soft Rains,' the book strikingly described the clash of cultures, as superior telepathic Martian civilization is ruthlessly destroyed by the greed of Earthmen. The planet of many dreams becomes a lifeless, dreadful place, littered with hot dog stands, empty Coke bottles and other witnesses to human banality. Those melancholically lyrical stories voice a protest against material civilization; gentle and deeply human, full of the poetry of small things, and yet bitingly satirical. Bradbury makes use of the traditional paraphernalia of sf – rockets, blasters, telepathy – but uses these devices to express moral concerns. He is the sf writer looking to the world outside the small boundaries of science fiction, interpreting sf for the general public. This is equally true of Bradbury's other major sf book, *The Illustrated Man*, a protest against the misuse of technology, and the standardization and regimentation of people. Often accused of being 'against' science, he has been misquoted as saying: 'I don't like what science is doing to the world. I think science is a good thing to escape from,' a charge Bradbury denies emphatically, correcting it to: 'I don't like what some people are doing with science in the world. I think that such people should be exposed and, if possible, combatted.'

Interested neither in science itself, nor even in the effects of science upon human life, he looks to its aesthetic and symbolic value in expressing human problems. Bradbury yearns for a lost world, a time of childhood and pre-technological innocence, and uses the modern trappings of science fiction to express traditional topics. This fact, together with his consummate artistry, has ensured his success among the general public. His fears are shared by many; his trauma of book-burning, treated so impressively in the dystopian novella *Fahrenheit 451* (the title refers to the temperature at which paper begins to burn), is a vivid warning to those who remember the past and are haunted by the thought that it might recur in the near future.

Ray Bradbury's 'illustrated man' and book-burners (in Fahrenheit 451*) reveal a hankering after a time long ago when signs and symbols – words and pictures – were not yet ousted by technology and 'progress'.*

The fabulous art of Hannes Bok

Of the many artists who have illustrated American sf magazines, three stand out most prominently: Frank R. Paul (1880–1963), Virgil Finlay (1914–71) and Hannes Bok (1914–64). Viennese-born Frank Paul's naive drawings of alien cities and extraterrestrial beings, huge machines and contraptions of the future, were eminently suited to the early days of magazine sf, with its crudely written literature of wonder. Virgil Finlay, best known as the illustrator of A. Merritt, is easily recognizable by the beauties he liked

to draw, their modesty characteristically protected by soap bubbles. His finely drawn work admirably met the requirements of fantasy and conveyed a mood of strangeness. But it was Hannes Bok who caught the fantastic spirit better than any other. His highly individual, stylized pictures, his gentle halftones, seem literally out of this world. In his paintings – which invariably suffered in print from poor reproduction – he tried to make what he called 'kodachromes of the impossible.' Barely able to eke out a subsistence from ill-paid work for the pulps (whose editors preferred simple, action-packed pictures), sometimes cheated by publishers, Bok led the life of a lonely artist, without ever gaining the recognition due his art. After his death, Emil Petaja, a long-time friend, set up the 'Bokanalia Foundation' in an attempt to collect Bok's work and keep it from dissolving with the crumbling pulp paper on which so much had been published. Several folios of Bok's art have appeared. A friend of Maxfield Parrish, Hannes Bok was also much admired by Ray Bradbury, who called him 'one of the best, yet least known, fantasy artists and illustrators of our time.' As a writer, Hannes Bok is less important, having been no more than a disciple of A. Merritt; two of his novels were recently reissued in paperback.

2001 – A Space Odyssey

'M-G-M doesn't know it yet, but they've footed the bill for the first ten-and-a-half-million-dollar religious film,' popular sf writer Arthur C. Clarke declared of Stanley Kubrick's film based on his script. Indeed, *2001* is a brilliant visual tour-de-force of space travel that gives its audience an almost religious experience, that cosmic feeling that sf fans like to call the 'sense of wonder.' It is a grandiose spectacle of the space age, full of hardware, its cast of characters so schematized that

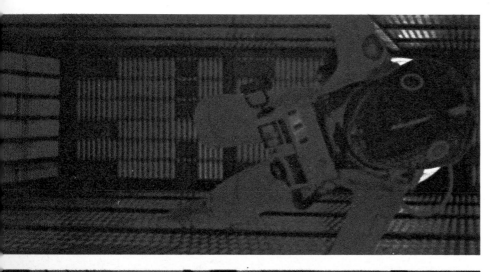

Stills from the Stanley Kubrick/MGM film production of Arthur C. Clarke's 2001.

the most human being in it happens to be the computer HAL 9000. The screenplay is based on Clarke's minor short story 'The Sentinel' (1950), from which the idea of the 'Monolith' was derived. The Kubrick-Clarke cooperation was at least partially due to the publicity that Clarke received after winning UNESCO's 1962 Kalinga Award for the popularization of science. In fact, Clarke's nonfiction has been far more important than his fiction, ever since *The Exploration of Space* was a

selection of the Book-of-the-Month Club in 1952.

Born in Somerset, England, on December 16, 1917, Clarke was an early member of the British Interplanetary Society founded in 1933. As a prophet he scored a remarkable hit with his article 'Extra-Terrestrial Relays' in the October 1945 issue of *Wireless World*, in which he first proposed the utilization of orbital satellites for global television. (The world has since learned how much money he

lost by failing to patent the idea.)

Like many other sf writers, Clarke began as a contributor to amateur sf magazines such as the British *Novae Terrae*. His fiction falls neatly into two categories: near-journalistic accounts of technological advances of the immediate future (*Prelude to Space*, 1951); and more poetic tales set in the distant future, such as *Against the Fall of Night*, written between 1937 and 1946, but not published until 1948, and *Childhood's End* (1952). The earlier

title transported readers into a super-city of the future, a paradise where the adventure has gone out of life – a warning that, to remain truly human, mankind must ever face new challenges. Similarly located in the far future was the mystical *Childhood's End*; in this novel guardian creatures from outer space resembling the classical image of the devil arrive on earth and put an end to war; all mankind is unified into a single super-intelligence, all recorded history having been but the childhood of the race awaiting this supreme moment. In *2001* similarly a 'Star-Child' of unspecified powers appears whose goals are unknown even to himself. 'But he would think of something,' as the lame punchline of the novel puts it.

(*Above*) Like many other sf authors, Arthur C. Clarke began his career with publication in the 'pulps.' (*Right*) An illustration by Hannes Bok for one of Clarke's early stories.

Buck Rogers, Superman, et al.

'A clean-cut, athletic, adventurous 20th century youth.' That's the fellow that earned science fiction the easy dismissal of 'That Buck Rogers stuff!' Succumbing to radio-active gas in an abandoned mine after 1918, Buck Rogers wakes in the 25th century, and soon has occasion to save a woman, a task often to be repeated when she has become his sweetheart. For there be Mongols who have conquered America, and there is 'Killer Kane', Buck's enemy, bent on world conquest. Written by Philip Francis Nowlan, and drawn by Dick Calkins, the first sf comic strip ever was adapted from two of Nowlan's novelettes in *Amazing Stories*: 'Armageddon – 2419 AD' (August 1928) and 'The Airlords of Han' (March 1929). Originally featuring 'Anthony' Rogers, the stories caught the eye of John Flint Dille, founder of the National Newspaper Syndicate of America. The strip originally followed the stories closely, but later included adventures on the moon, Martian invasions, and an expedition to sunken Atlantis. 'Buck Rogers' was the first comic strip to employ sf devices such as rockets, blasters and expeditions to other planets; its influence can hardly be overrated.

The next futuristic strip of importance to enter the scene was 'Flash Gordon,' the creation of Alexander ('Alex') Raymond (1909–56), perhaps the most versatile of all the great comic-strip artists. Gifted with an almost apocalyptic imagination, Raymond, working for King Features Syndicate, pitted his heroes – Flash himself, his sweetheart Dale and Professor Zarkov – against the villainous Emperor Ming, ruler of the planet Mongo. Set against marvellous backgrounds – a Kingdom of Shadows, an undersea city – absolute good fights against evil incarnate.

Superman, almost invulnerable, able to fly through the air, and endowed with X-ray vision and other useful attributes, is the last survivor of the blown-up planet Krypton; his vocation is the eternal fight against the evil-doers of Metropolis. Without his smart cape and uniform he is the reporter Clark Kent, despised by young girl reporter Lois Lane, who never suspects that this fumbling weakling is no other than the Man of Steel himself, the epitome of masculinity. 'Superman' is the creation of the sf fans Jerry Siegel (author) and Joe Shuster (artist); although turned down by syndicates for five years, it was a huge success from the beginning when it finally appeared in *Action Comics* in 1938, offering the reader easy wish fulfillment, while Superman's fake personality Clark Kent, the common man as seen by Superman, allowed a focussing of sympathy. Superman spawned forth Superwoman, Superboy and Superdog, and sometimes teamed up with 'Batman'. Like Superman, hooded 'Batman' is 'a mysterious and adventurous figure fighting for righteousness and apprehending the wrong-doer, in his lone battle against the evil forces of society' (Episode One of 'Batman', *Detective Comics*, May 1939). Batman, however, is a most vulnerable hero and not a superhuman one, having to rely more than Superman on his wits. Drawn by artist Bob Kane, Batman lives in a macabre world of mystery, a realm of long shadows, crudely drawn, yet compelling.

Jean-Claude Forest's 'Barbarella', Guy Pellaert and Pascal Thomas' 'Pravda' and Guy Pellaert and Pierre Bartier's 'Jodelle' finally have given sf a number of amazon-like super-women, an answer to the male world of the superheroes, where women are just objects to be rescued.

This whole field has been spiritedly attacked by psychologists and psychiatrists like Gershon Legman (*Love and Death*, 1949) and Frederic Wertheim (*Seduction of the Innocent*, 1954) for their supposedly harmful effects on young people, but others find the not-so-funny 'funnies' the truest expression of the American way of life.

(Below) Superman's unearthly powers have never been a safeguard against the emotional problems of ordinary earthlings! (Opposite) Batman about to go into action.

Secondary universes and magic lands

(*Opposite*) *The frontispiece, by Keith Henderson, to the 1967 edition of E. R. Eddison's* The Worm Ouroborus, *first published in 1926.*

Epics, sagas and fairy tales have long offered the ingredients for the 'secondary universe' story, a subgenre of fantasy represented by stories located in imaginary lands, where magic works, fabulous beasts dwell, and as likely as not contending forces, that of absolute good and that of absolute evil, meet in battle. The originator of this kind of fiction is said to be William Morris (1834–96), that highly talented designer and writer, who longed for the simplicity of the Middle Ages. From translating sagas, Morris went on to write novels such as *The Wood Beyond the World* (1895), *The Well at the World's End* (1896) and *The Water of the Wondrous Isles* (1897), in which he employed a beautifully simple and archaic language to describe deeds

wrought in quasi-medieval realms. His direct literary heir was Edward John Moreton Drax Plunkett, the eighteenth Baron Dunsany (1878–1957), who wrote strange vignettes set at the world's edge or *Beyond the Fields We Know* – the title of one modern anthology of his oddly-titled stories ('The Fortress Unvanquishable Save for Sacnoth,' 'The Distressing Tale of Thangobrind the Jeweller'). His singing prose is collected in *Time and the Gods* (1906), *A Dreamer's Tales* (1910), *The Book of Wonder* (1912) and *Tales of Three Hemispheres* (1919).

Perhaps the most splendorous 'secondary universe' novel ever written is Eric Rücker Eddison's (1882–1945) *The Worm Ouroboros* (1922). Flaming with high rhetoric and grandiose des-

criptive passages, it adopts the topos of the heroic quest, and of warfare between the classical antagonists – in this case, the lords of Demonland and King Gorice XII of Witchland. Eddison extols the virtues of nobility, courage and loyalty even in the face of inevitable doom; he followed this somber epic with the Zimiamvian trilogy *Mistress of Mistresses* (1935), *A Fish Dinner in Memison* (1941) and the unfinished *Menzentian Gate* (1958).

Among contemporary imaginary world stories none has had more success than those of Professor John Ronald Reuel Tolkien (1892–1973). In 1937 he published a children's book called *The Hobbit, or, There and Back Again*. Tolkien introduced a society of sympathetic creatures, the habit-forming hobbits, of the same order as elves, trolls or goblins. The further history of the hobbits and the human-kind inhabiting the realm known as Middle-earth is narrated in the *Lords of the Ring* trilogy (*The Fellowship of the Ring*, 1954; *The Two Towers*, 1954 and *The Return of the King*, 1955). In paperback the trilogy became a pheno-menal success, selling millions of copies. Rich in earthbound details and mythic lore, full of adventure, this gigantic fairy tale for grownups seems to satisfy its readers' longing for a world closer to nature, homely in its fashions and languages, and with clear-cut loyalties and simple delineated moral problems.

More concerned with sheer enter-tainment by the route of fast-moving and direct action are several American authors of 'sub-creation' (Tolkien's phrase): Robert E. Howard (1906–36), C. A. Smith (1893–1961), Fritz Leiber (1910–) are the best known of these. Howard created a number of barbarian heroes: King Kull, Bran Mak Morn, or Conan the Cimmerian, a man of simple lusts and disposition who be-lieves there is no problem that cannot be solved by his mighty broadsword. In the 'Hyborian Age' there is none supreme to him, neither king nor wizard, nor is he easily tamed by a damsel. Yet the cord that once tied the creator of vigorous Conan to his mother is still so strong at age 30 that he blows out his brains when he learns she is dying. Clark Ashton Smith, a painter and poet, wrote decadent, bizarrely exotic tales of wizardry in the far past (in *Atlantis* and *Hyperborea*), the medi-eval *Averoigne*, the infinitely remote future of the Earth (*Zothique*) or on other planets (*Xiccarph*). Smith writes a colorful prose embellished with rare and obsolete words; his books are preoccupied with death and decay, his manner tortuously ironical. Fritz Leiber's two lowly rogues Fafhrd and the Gray Mouser, characterized by a sly and dry humor, have waged their adventures through five collections of short stories and novellas.

First contact: forms of life in outer space

What kind of life will Man encounter in outer space? Will they be intelligent beings, friends or foes?

One solution was proposed by Murray Leinster's short story 'First Contact' (1945), in which a distrustful Earth crew exchanges space ships with a group of equally distrustful aliens. In English-language sf, extraterrestrials come in all varieties: good, bad and indifferent, superior guardians of mankind, the classic BEM's (Bug-Eyed Monsters) of the space opera, or the aliens of stories like Stanley G. Weinbaum's 'A Martian Odyssey' (*Wonder Stories*, July 1934) or Heinlein's 'The Star Beast' (1954). In the socialist countries, sf writers argue that beings who have attained a technology capable of inter-stellar flight will have shed the burden of war. Reason will triumph among the stars, if we are to believe stories such as Ivan Efremov's 'The Heart of the Serpent,' which contains an explicit attack on Leinster's story.

Sometimes aliens ignore humans, or exterminate them like so much vermin – as in Thomas M. Disch's *The Genocides* – or treat them like pet animals – as in French author Edward de Capoulet-Junac's *Pallas, or The Tribulation*. Sometimes contact is altogether impossible, as in Katherine MacLean's 'Pictures Don't Lie,' in which the long-awaited visitors from space turn out to be so small that they drown in a puddle. And Stanisław Lem argues that the physical form of aliens may be so different from anything we know that no common point of reference will exist – as in Lem's novel *Solaris*, in which the humans are unable to determine whether or not the ocean on the planet Solaris is intelligent.

A STREET & SMITH PUBLICATION

ASTOUNDING
Science fiction
REG. U. S. PAT. OFF.

MAY 1945

25 CENTS

FIRST CONTACT
BY MURRAY LEINSTER

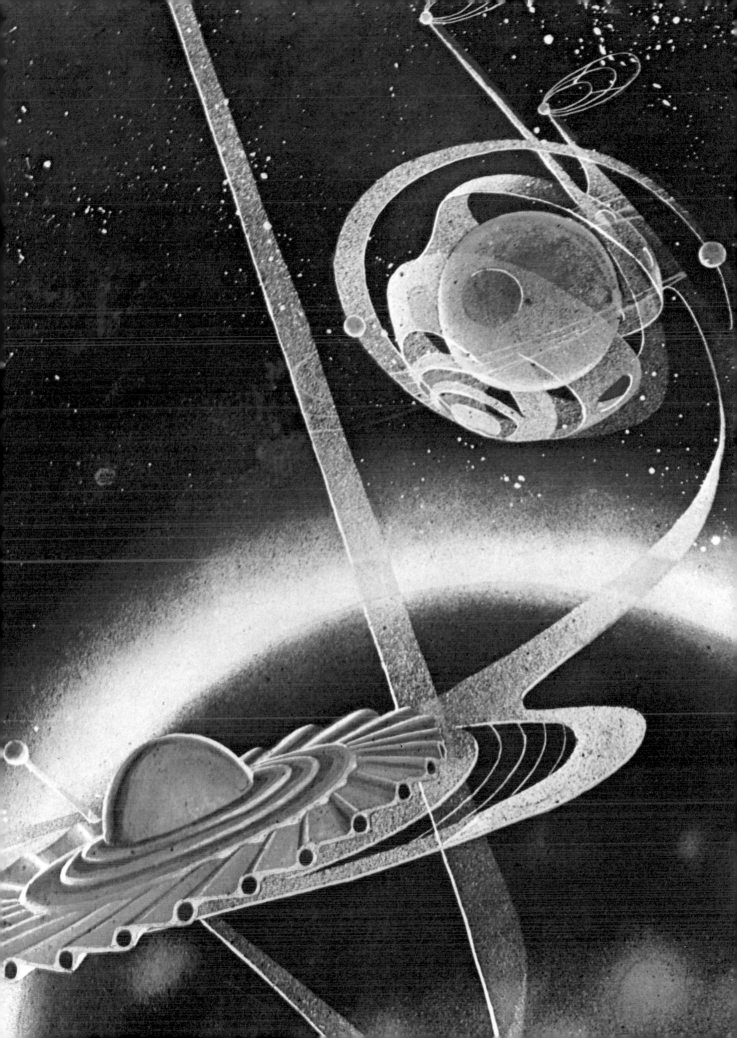

Why there is no sex in science fiction

For a long time, sex in sf was restricted to the beautiful daughters of mad scientists, seemingly destined to be devoured by some bug-eyed monster or to be tortured in a horror-chamber. Now, of course, the mad scientists survive only in sf movies. Nevertheless, science fiction continues to be a man's world, and those female characters who appear in it are weak creatures, very much in need of protection, wholly helpless to act on their own account; even female writers present them in this light. The one author most often cited as exploring aspects of love in his stories, Theodore Sturgeon, has merely adapted soap opera to science fiction, presenting schmaltz and tears rather than genuine feeling. Many of his stories follow the pattern of 'the man who learned loving', the man dis-

THE SECRET DREAM
OF EVERY MAN WAS HIS —
UNLIMITED OPPORTUNITY,
INEXHAUSTABLE ABILITY.

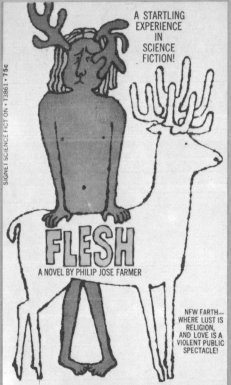

A STARTLING
EXPERIENCE
IN
SCIENCE
FICTION!

NEW EARTH—
WHERE LUST IS
RELIGION,
AND LOVE IS A
VIOLENT PUBLIC
SPECTACLE!

trustful of love who finally arrives at some kind of fulfillment, presented in rosy sentimental colors. These stories transmit the uncomfortable feeling that the author is not so much conveying an experience to the reader, as trying to convince himself that love, after all, is not something sinful. The immense popularity of Sturgeon's stories is a sure indication of the emotional immaturity of the whole sf genre. Interpersonal and sexual relationships in sf are almost invariably presented in a mechanical way, devoid of spontaneity, especially where the authors claim to fight against taboos. The work of Robert Silverberg, Harlan Ellison and Norman Spinrad offers typical examples.

The one exception in science fiction who has often dealt in a freer way with

Sf authors may generally avoid sex in their plots, but the details on these pages make it clear that illustrators of science fiction do not feel the same reticence.

sexual problems is Philip José Farmer (born January 26, 1918), although he too is more adept at describing vividly xenobiological oddities than presenting psychological insights. When his novel *The Lovers* was published in *Startling Stories*, August 1952, it caused a storm of controversy. On the planet Ozagen (Oz again), an earthman from a repressive theocracy falls in love with a 'lalitha', a parasitic being grown into the semblance of a woman. What for most other writers would have served as the starting point for a xenophobic horror-story, Farmer turned into a tender love-story, which extends man's sexual activities to other species. Other samples of his method, often coupled with Freudian insights, are to be found in the stories of his collection *Strange Relations* (1960), and a novel of the fertility rites of the future (*Flesh*, 1960), as well as some hard-core pornography offering a fatal combination of sex and sadism. In *A Feast Unknown* (1969), the Apeman and Doc Caliban (the pulp hero, Doc Savage) appear as characters. It is typical that when the penis as a secret weapon proved commercially unprofitable, Farmer continued the book in two 'clean' novels, *Lord of the Tree* and *The Mad Goblin* (1970). In our culture, sex is always the first thing to go; the brutalities are allowed to survive.

The cyclopean mad scientist obviously has wicked intentions towards his terrified – but modest – victim.

EXOTIC · PEPPY · EXCITING

New **Mystery Adventures** 15c

December

Eye of the Fiend

Canyon of Doom

HAROLD F. CRUICKSHANK

Blaire

Sf on TV

'To explore strange new worlds, to seek out new civilizations, to boldly go where no man has gone before': that is the mission of the U.S.Starship *Enterprise*, a 947-feet-long saucer-shaped 190,000-ton military space cruiser manned by a racially integrated crew of 430 persons, one third of them women. Commander of the ship propelled by anti-matter motors and 'space warp' is Captain James T. Kirk, a Horatio Hornblower of outer space; in charge of all scientific departments aboard the space ship is Mr Spock, a green-blooded alien with slightly pointed ears that give him the sly look of a devil. Mr Spock is the son of an Earth woman and a man from the planet Vulcan, where people are strictly governed by logic, suppressing all emotion. At first frowned upon by the executives of NBC-TV network, this first alien regular in a TV programme proved by far the most popular character in *Star Trek*, that unusual 'Wagon Train to the Stars' TV series conceived and produced by Gene Rodenberry, who himself wrote some of the scripts. One of the best of the scripts was Rodenberry's pilot for the series – 'The Menagerie' – in which a castaway girl is rescued from tele-pathic alien monsters on a dying planet. *Star Trek* adopted the convenient sf frame of galactic empires and explor-ation out among the stars, which allowed it to combine the advantages of a series with the more usual TV form of sf collections: for in an infinity of worlds, some should be expected to be similar to Earth, thus helping to keep

Mr Spock and companions – from the television serial Star Trek.

production costs down. This freedom to present almost anything on the screen eventually led to the deterioration of the series, which drew too many parallels to the Earth's past, offering historical adventures and gangster and war stories thinly disguised as science fiction by the introduction of time-travel or discoveries on all too Earth-like planets.

More astonishing than the things offered on the TV screen were the reactions provoked by the series. When, after running for two seasons, it was announced that the series would be dropped, the network, according to an NBC press release dated March 4, 1968, had received no less than 114,667 pieces of mail in support of *Star Trek* from December of the previous year up to that date! As 'Star Trekkies' (the most rabid fans) will have it, one million letters were eventually received by NBC. Soon afterwards, after having been assigned a less suitable time spot, the series was nevertheless dropped, but the phenomenon of *Star Trek* fandom continues unabated, with 'I Grok Spock' buttons, magazines de-

voted solely to writings on *Star Trek*, a first *Star Trek* convention in January 1972, attended by over 3,000 people, and so on.

Outstanding among TV sf productions were those produced by the British Broadcasting Corporation between 1953 and 1960, especially Nigel Kneale's striking sf horror plays *Quatermass*, *Quatermass II* and *Quatermass and the Pit*. American series like *Lost in Space* (1967), *Voyage to the Bottom of the Sea* (1966), *The Invaders* (1967) or the BBC serial *Dr Who*, offered only stock situations, hoary space opera and cheap melodrama; no better were a militaristic German series *Space Patrol Orion* and a French serial scripted by the notorious Jacques Bergier. Only *The Outer Limits*, produced between 1964 and 1965, fully explored the visual possibilities of real science fiction. Too sophisticated for a mass-audience, it was, however, never a commercial success. Still more sophisticated are the short TV films produced in countries like Poland, Czechoslovakia, Yugoslavia or Hungary, where TV directors do not

have to worry about selling the sponsor's products or achieving a good audience rating, and so can experiment freely. A good example of such a TV film is that created by *Ashes and Diamonds* producer Andrzej Wajda, *Roly Poly* ('Przekładaniec'), based on a script by Stanisław Lem, an amusing story of a racing car driver who has undergone so many transplants that it can no longer be determined which persons have contributed to his make-up.

(Above) Still from a Hungarian sf television production.

Quatermass *and* Dr Who *both enjoyed extension into another dimension of communication – still earthbound but progressive.*

Science fiction in the Soviet Union

To a greater extent than American sf, Soviet science fiction is a collective phenomenon embracing a common vision, a bright picture of a better future dominated by the ethics of cooperation. The standard brand of Soviet sf is given to an enthusiasm for hardware and its only conflicts are those between 'the good and the better,' as the Strugatski brothers once remarked upon a phase of their own work. Sever Gansovski, Anatoli Dneprov, Gennadi Gor, Genrikh Altov and Ilya Varshavski are among the better writers, but the most popular novel of Soviet utopianism to date is Ivan Efremov's (1907–) *Andromeda Nebula*. Published in 1957–58 against initial opposition, it subsequently took Soviet readers by storm and sold by the millions. *The Andromeda Nebula* envisions an ideal Communist commonwealth in the year 3000, the era of the 'Great Ring,' a communication net connecting all sentient beings in the universe. Efremov's novel combines the picture of a classless, idyllic Earth with a love story across the gulf of 280 light-years to the star Epsilon Tucanae in a high adventure of astronautics. The new ethics is exemplified by an experiment that furthers human knowledge at the expense of several lives, thus raising the ancient question as to whether the ends justify the means. Though it has its defects as a novel, *The Andromeda Nebula* is the most ambitious Russian utopian novel to date, and far outdistances Efremov's later effort, *The Hour of the Bull* (1970). It is paralleled perhaps only by Stanisław Lem's early novel *The Magellan Nebula* (1955).

Two acknowledged masters of sf in the U.S.S.R. are the Strugatski

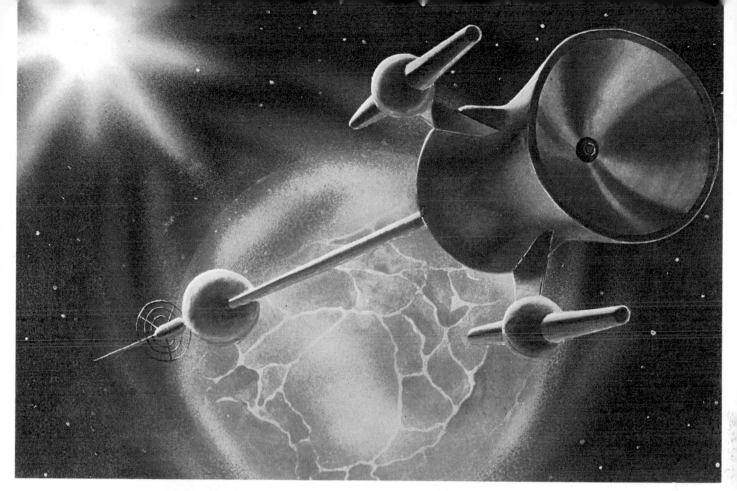

(Opposite) Soviet illustrator Andrei Sokolov's conception of a space ship from Earth in its descent through the carbon dioxide-filled atmosphere of Venus. (Above) Sokolov's Space Ship Passing a Double Star. *(Right) Cover illustration to the German edition of the Strugatskis'* The Second Invasion of the Martians.

brothers, who write only as a team: Boris Strugatski (born 1933) is an astronomer, a mathematician at the observatory of Pulkovo, while Arkadi (born 1925) is a linguist, Japanologist and translator. After early stories and novels such as *The Country of Purple Clouds, The Apprentices* and *Far Rainbow*, the brothers came into their own with *Hard to be a God* (1964). In this successful adoption of the picaresque adventure novel, the Strugatskis probe deeply into the problems of the autonomy of historical development and the justification of intervention. The hero of the novel, Rumata, is one of the graduates from the Earth Institute of Experimental History sent to a feudal medieval world thousands of parsecs away to survey local developments. Conditions in Arkanar, the principal empire on that world, turn from bad to worse, erupting into mass-pogroms and civil wars. Rumata learns in a series of trying adventures that he cannot improve the situation of the people, who must go their own way. The novel is a sharp attack against oppression, tyranny, social indifference and human stupidity, presented within a framework of lively and inventive narrative. Less successful is *The Inhabited Island* (1969), a return to the theme of oppression and manipulation by supposedly benevolent 'fathers'; it is a thinly disguised attack on Stalinism, welded to a superman plot.

In *Hard to be a God, The Second Invasion of the Martians* (1967), *The Snail on the Slope* (1966–68) and *The Fairy Tale of the Troika* (1968) the Strugatskis have turned Soviet science fiction into a sharp tool for social criticism. The Martians of *The Second Invasion* require no heat rays or battle equipment to subjugate Earth, but merely a stream of rumors, local intrigue and unbroken corruption. *The Fairy Tale of the Troika*, published in the Siberian journal *Angara*, presents a bureaucratic triumvirate in a grotesque never-never land, battling against assorted strange phenomena. Close to Kafka is the black parable *The Snail on the Slope*, where the universe is presented as a swampy forest, pitted against a bureaucratic monster, the 'Forest Study and Exploitation Auth-

ority.' Following in the footsteps of writers like Gogol or Bulgakov, the Strugatskis have made a genuinely original contribution to science fiction and shown that Soviet sf, where it is aware of the great tradition of Russian literature, belongs to the top order of fantastic literature.

(*Below*) *A still from the Soviet film production of* The Andromeda Nebula, *and illustrations to* The Snail on the Slope.

The literature of cataclysm

Mary Shelley's novel *The Last Man* (1826) appeared to a contemporary critic as 'the product of a diseased imagination and a polluted taste, which described the ravages of the plague in such minute detail that the result was not a picture but a lecture in anatomy' (as paraphrased by Elizabeth Nitchie in her book *Mary Shelley*). What so revolted the public who had favourably received the earlier *Frankenstein* – the imagining of the end of the world, or at least the end of mankind – is not so remote and improbable an idea to us, to

whom the complete obliteration of all human life is, in William Faulkner's phrase, a possibility 'so long sustained by now that men can even bear it.' Atomic doom, a real danger since World War II, has given the theme an upsurge in recent times, but an apocalyptic imagination has always strongly colored science fiction and formed a subgenre in it long before the extermination of life on this planet became an ever-present threat. Undoubtedly shaped to a great extent by subconscious desires, the longing to see the world go up in

flames has always held a special attraction for sf writers, and they have devised an amazing number of imaginative ways to achieve the prospect both feared and longingly embraced. *The Scarlet Plague* (1915) by Jack London (1876–1916) recaptured the Romantic feeling of 'Weltschmerz' generated by Mary Shelley, and as the title of his story suggests, the chosen method of doing away with mankind is similar to hers. In the manner of the biblical paradigm, the world was flooded, among others, in popular American astronomer

JULY

25¢

Fantastic
Novels
MAGAZINE

A FAMED
FANTASY CLASSIC

**THE
SECOND
DELUGE**

THE STORY OF A
WORLD IN CHAOS

by **GARRETT
P. SERVISS**

JUNE

Famous

FANTASTIC
Mysteries

25¢

THE PURPLE CLOUD

ONE OF THE
WORLD'S MOST
FAMOUS FANTASIES
by **M. P. SHIEL**

Garrett P. Serviss's (1851–1929) *The Second Deluge* (1911), in which a latter-day Noah embarks on a metal ark to save a small number of people and animals, and in Sydney Fowler Wright's (1874–) *Deluge* (1928), with its sequel *Dawn* (1929). *Dawn* points to a feature common to many of the disaster stories: not only does the world or civilization come to an end, but this end also offers the chance for a new beginning, a purging, an opportunity to build a better world from the ruins. This is the theme of *Earth Abides* (1949) by George R. Stewart, one of the most moving of all ecological catastrophe stories, and of *When Worlds Collide* (1932) and *After Worlds Collide* (1933) by Edwin Balmer and Philip Wylie (1902–1971), where the earth collides with a cosmic wanderer, and only a few people escape to another world in a rocket. Astronomical cataclysms were described earlier by H. G. Wells in 'In the Days of the Comet' (1906) and especially in his classic short story 'The Star' (1897). Wells was a leader in the aesthetics of destruction as in any sf theme he ever touched upon in his works. Although other people joined in the game, the world destruction story has always remained a British preserve, from the classics to modern times. In *The Purple Cloud* (1901), Matthew Phipps Shiel (1866–1947) has humanity wiped out by a deadly gas; in *The Hopkins Manuscript* (1939), R. C. Sherriff has the moon fall on Europe. John Christopher (Christopher Sam Youd) writes of *The Death of Grass* (1956), and in John Wyndham's *The Day of the Triffids* (1951) mankind is blinded by an accident and then stalked by poisonous mobile plants. In Wyndham's *The Kraken Wakes* (1953), interstellar monsters hide in the ocean depths. In writer after writer and book after book, mankind is drowned, grilled, frozen, crystallized, burned.

The shock of August 8, 1945, the 'day the world ended', has led to a spate of novels envisioning atomic doom or describing post-atomic societies, savage and primitive. The warning has been so often repeated, and so often exploited for cheap eschatological thrills, that it is sometimes hard to take such stories seriously any longer. Of the many novels of atomic holocaust, Nevil

Shute's *On the Beach* (1957) is probably the best known, sentimental as it is. On the screen, the most effective treatment was Stanley Kubrick's black comedy *Dr Strangelove or How I Learned to Stop Worrying and Love the Bomb* (1964), based on the novel *Red Alert* by Peter George. With films like *Seven Days in May* or *Fail Safe*, based on best-selling novels by Fletcher-Knebel and Burdick-Wheeler, 'the megadunit' (Brian W. Aldiss's term) has developed a ritual of atomic blackmail, a vocabulary of 'overkill,' 'atomic patt,' 'megatons,' 'red telephones' and 'hot lines' between the Kremlin and the Pentagon, in manoeuvres to save man from killing himself with his frightening arsenal of doomsday machines.

The end of the world may come from vegetable disorientation (The Day of the Triffids), *interplanetary confusion* (When Worlds Collide) *and atomic holocaust* (On The Beach).

Science fiction, above all a prospective form of fiction concerned with the immediate present in terms of the future rather than the past, requires narrative techniques that reflect its subject-matter. To date almost all writers, including myself, fall to the ground because they fail to realise that the principal narrative technique of retrospective fiction, the sequential and consequential narrative, based as it is on an already set of events and relationships, is wholly unsuited to create the images of a future that has as yet made no concession to us.

(J. G. Ballard,
'Notes from Nowhere,' *New Worlds* 167)

The 'new wave'

Sf illustration has kept pace with the increasing sophistication of its authors.

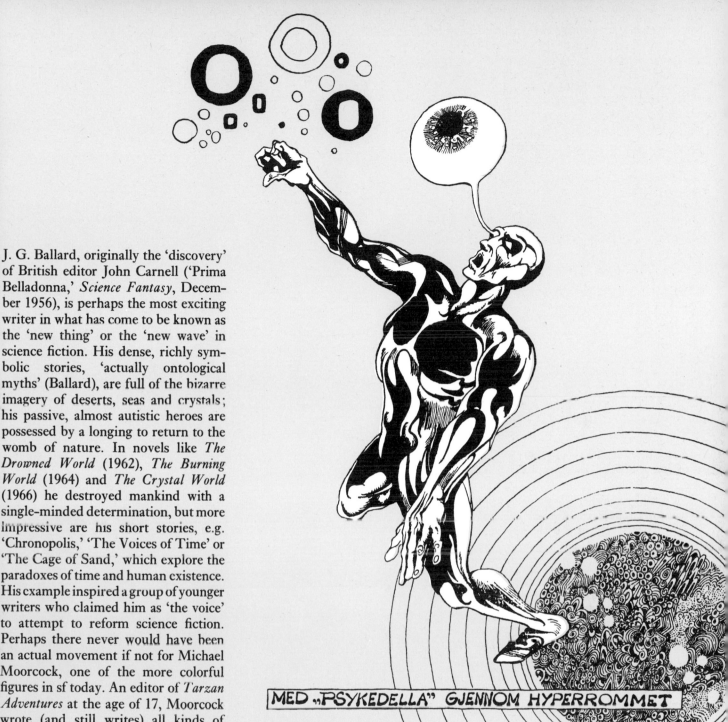

MED „PSYKEDELLA" GJENNOM HYPERROMMET

J. G. Ballard, originally the 'discovery' of British editor John Carnell ('Prima Belladonna,' *Science Fantasy*, December 1956), is perhaps the most exciting writer in what has come to be known as the 'new thing' or the 'new wave' in science fiction. His dense, richly symbolic stories, 'actually ontological myths' (Ballard), are full of the bizarre imagery of deserts, seas and crystals; his passive, almost autistic heroes are possessed by a longing to return to the womb of nature. In novels like *The Drowned World* (1962), *The Burning World* (1964) and *The Crystal World* (1966) he destroyed mankind with a single-minded determination, but more impressive are his short stories, e.g. 'Chronopolis,' 'The Voices of Time' or 'The Cage of Sand,' which explore the paradoxes of time and human existence. His example inspired a group of younger writers who claimed him as 'the voice' to attempt to reform science fiction. Perhaps there never would have been an actual movement if not for Michael Moorcock, one of the more colorful figures in sf today. An editor of *Tarzan Adventures* at the age of 17, Moorcock wrote (and still writes) all kinds of popular literature, including sf; thus it came as something of a surprise when the author of the popular 'Elric' sword and sorcery series took the editorial chair of the British publication *New Worlds* (No. 142, May–June 1964) to proclaim a new 'literature for the Space Age.' Moorcock encouraged literary experiment, freedom from the formulas of magazine sf and wider thematic and stylistic scope. Engaged from the beginning in a polemic against fans and writers who felt that sf was being threatened by the 'new wave,'

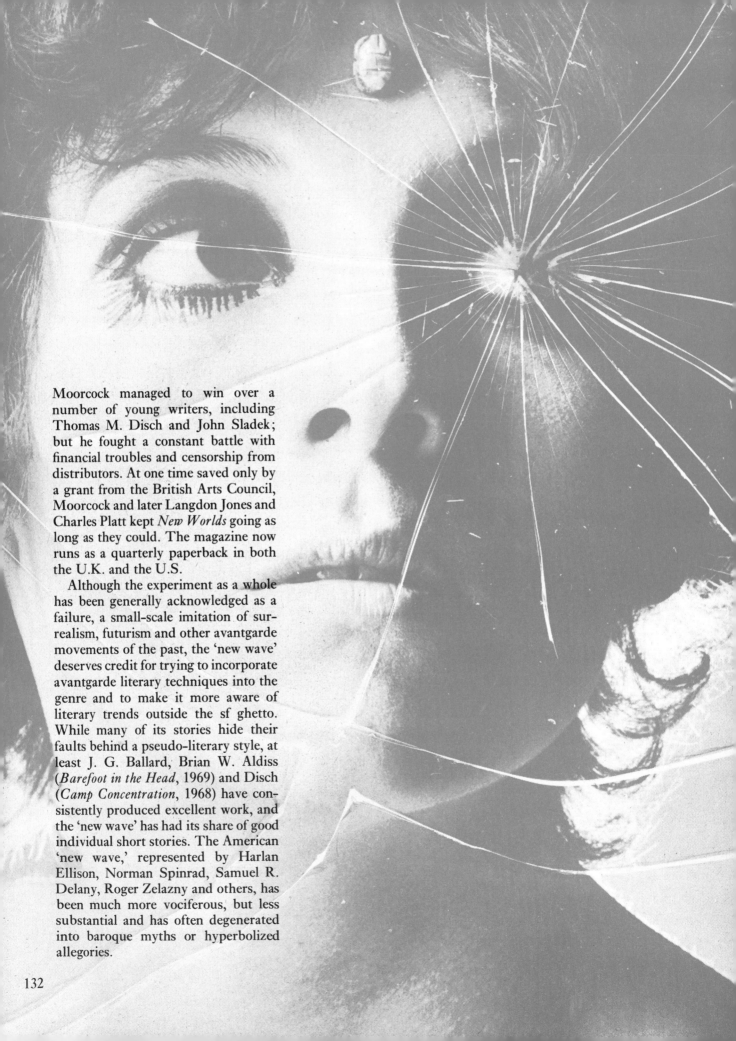

Moorcock managed to win over a number of young writers, including Thomas M. Disch and John Sladek; but he fought a constant battle with financial troubles and censorship from distributors. At one time saved only by a grant from the British Arts Council, Moorcock and later Langdon Jones and Charles Platt kept *New Worlds* going as long as they could. The magazine now runs as a quarterly paperback in both the U.K. and the U.S.

Although the experiment as a whole has been generally acknowledged as a failure, a small-scale imitation of surrealism, futurism and other avantgarde movements of the past, the 'new wave' deserves credit for trying to incorporate avantgarde literary techniques into the genre and to make it more aware of literary trends outside the sf ghetto. While many of its stories hide their faults behind a pseudo-literary style, at least J. G. Ballard, Brian W. Aldiss (*Barefoot in the Head*, 1969) and Disch (*Camp Concentration*, 1968) have consistently produced excellent work, and the 'new wave' has had its share of good individual short stories. The American 'new wave,' represented by Harlan Ellison, Norman Spinrad, Samuel R. Delany, Roger Zelazny and others, has been much more vociferous, but less substantial and has often degenerated into baroque myths or hyperbolized allegories.

(*Opposite*) *A photographic illustration to Gretchen Haapenen's 'The Pieces of the Game' in* New Worlds (*No. 184*). (*Centre*) *R. Glyn Jones' illustration to Ian Watson's 'Roof Garden Under Saturn' (*New Worlds, *No. 195*) *superimposed on Dean's illustration to J. G. Ballard's 'The Killing Ground' (No. 188*).

133

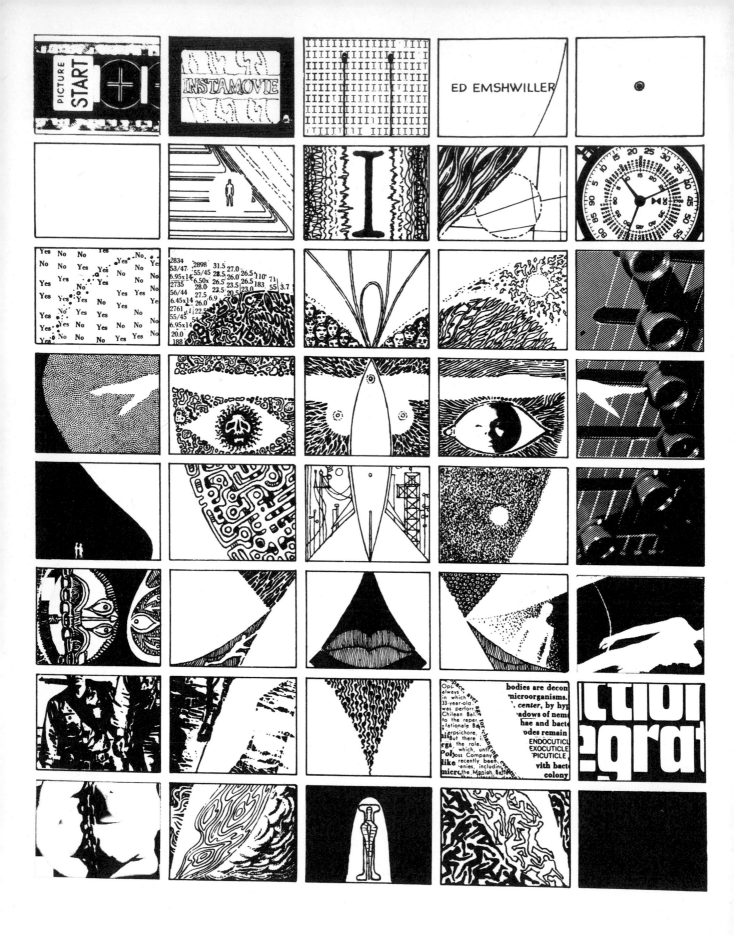

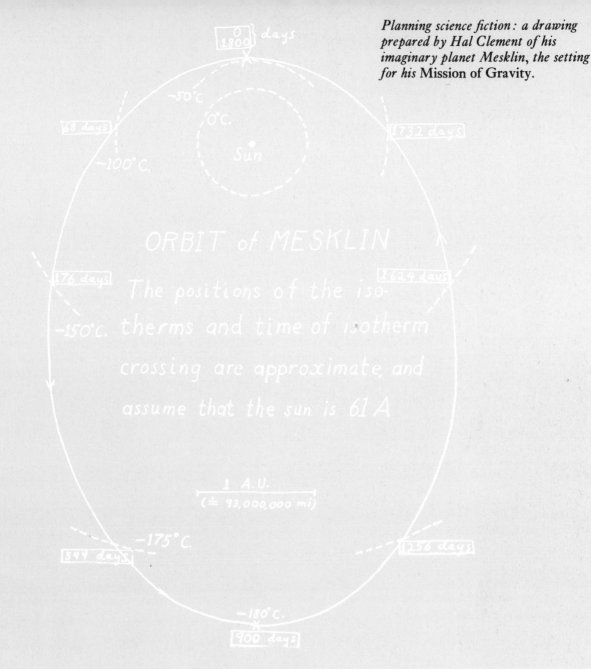

Planning science fiction: a drawing prepared by Hal Clement of his imaginary planet Mesklin, the setting for his Mission of Gravity.

The positions of the isotherms and time of isotherm crossing are approximate, and assume that the sun is 61 A

Hard sf

Hard science fiction denotes a kind of story in which the scientific element is central and not just tagged on as an ornament. It represents an essential part of sf, with an importance far exceeding its numerical strength, and can be looked on as the continuation of the Vernian tradition. It is hardly surprising that the actual scientists among sf writers have always contributed a good deal to it. One of these was John Taine, a leading American sf writer of the 'twenties and 'thirties. His real name was Eric Temple Bell (1883–1960), and he was one of the world's foremost mathematicians, a professor at the California Institute of Technology and a recipient of many honors and awards. Of his more than a dozen novels, *The Time Stream*, first published in the magazine *Wonder Stories*, December 1931–March 1932, is especially remarkable as one of the first stories to develop the concept of cyclical universes, presenting time as a flow, and speculating on the nature of time and entropy. Many of John Taine's books deal with biological

themes and evolution: *Before the Dawn* (1934) transports the reader back to the Saurian Age; in *The Greatest Adventure* (1929), an expedition in the Antarctic discovers primeval beasts; and in *The Iron Star* (1930) rays cause a retrograde evolution, turning men into beasts. Many of these novels follow the Vernian and 'lost race' patterns of journeys into remote parts of the Earth, where strange phenomena and even stranger beings are encountered.

In more recent times, the outstanding example of 'hard science fiction' is *The Black Cloud* (1957) by Fred Hoyle, one of our leading contemporary astronomers. How communication is established with a gigantic cosmic cloud approaching the solar system and threatening to swallow it, makes up a thoughtful story that has never received the appreciation it deserves. This is probably the reason why Fred Hoyle,

(1961), Kalinga Prize winner Arthur C. Clarke has written level-headed, sober and almost reportorial accounts of the first flight into space and life on the moon and Mars in the near future.

More grandiose is the panoramic view in James Blish's Okie series, the *Cities in Flight* tetralogy. After the invention of longevity drugs and an anti-gravity drive, mass became irrelevant for space-travel, and whole cities took off into space on their rock-beds, becoming either modern hoboes seeking work in space, or turning to piracy. Buttressed with superficial references to Oswald Spengler's *Decline of the West*, Blish's novels *They Shall Have Stars* (1957), *A Life for the Stars* (1962), *Earthman, Come Home* (1955) and *The Triumph of Time* (1958) form a cosmic future history, spanning the next two thousand years in our galaxy and the next. Full of fights between galactic good and bad guys, and ending in total cataclysm as our universe collides with a universe of anti-matter, this super-galactic epic really is a

continuation of the tradition of space opera writing in the manner of E. E. Smith and John W. Campbell, Jr, who suggested that Blish turn one story into a series. That this form of adventure novel is still viable is confirmed by the success of Larry Niven's *Known Space* series. In his Hugo- and Nebula-winning novel *Ringworld* (1970), he dazzles the reader with an off-shot of a Dyson sphere, a cylindrical world, but uses the fascinating background only for the usual sf derring-do.

Less spectacular but more solid are the scientific puzzles set up by Hal Clement for his heroes. The 'Whirligig World' Mesklin of his novel *Mission of Gravity* (1953) is an ultradense planet with a gravity of 3 g. at the equator and nearly 700 g. at the poles, carefully calculated. Clement explained in an article in *Astounding Science Fiction*, June 1953, how he arrived at the figures for Mesklin, where Earthmen, with the help of natives, have to secure the information contained in a rocket probe crashed at the pole.

(Opposite) Two illustrations from the popular magazines showing the emphasis on technology in hard sf. (Below) Illustration for Clement's Mission of Gravity.

sometimes in collaboration with his son Geoffrey, went on to write a number of stock adventure yarns, which are remarkable neither for scientific accurateness nor for narrative vigor.

In books such as *Prelude to Space* (1951), *Seeds of Mars* (1951), *Earthlight* (1951) or *A Fall of Moondust*

Sf achievements in . . .

COPYRIGHTED
BY GEO MELIES 1906
PARIS NEW YORK

France . . .

Three varied examples of the French contribution to science fiction: (below) a scene from the Méliès film A Visit to the Sirens of Neptune, *1906; (right)* The Planet of the Apes *was based on a fantasy novel by Pierre Boulle; (right below) the Roger Vadim sf film* Barbarella, *based on a comic-strip heroine, 1969.*

After the U.S.S.R., France has the most vigorous field of native sf talent in Europe. Not only is science fiction published by 'respectable' houses such as Calmann-Lévy, Robert Laffont, Albin Michel and Editions Denoël, but publishers can boast a considerable body of original French sf and a number of regularly producing writers. In more than 250 issues, the magazine *Fiction* – basically a French edition of the American *Magazine of Fantasy and Science Fiction*, but which also features original work – has published some 700 French sf stories, some of admirable quality. Writers like Gérard Klein (who is also a noted critic and editor), Jacques Sternberg (a Belgian published mainly in France), Nathalie Charles-Henneberg, René Barjavel, J. P. Andrevon and Daniel Walther are modern representatives of French science fiction; many lesser space operas have been issued by the publishing house Fleuve Noir.

French sf is more romantic than cerebral, with a strong tendency toward mysticism and pseudo-science.

(Predictably enough, the most popular foreign sf author in France is Van Vogt.) Fairly typical of mass-appeal French sf is René Barjavel's bestseller *The Ice People* (*La Nuit des Temps*, 1968), a bitter-sweet romantic novel about a couple from lost Atlantis, frozen survivors of a world torn asunder by atomic war, who awaken in the future. Speculations about time and space are combined with suggestions of a forgotten super-science; nor is a warning against the misuse of atomic power lacking; and melodrama is provided by evil machinations against a glorious love-affair.

The classic tradition of literary science fiction, represented by such names as J. H. Rosny *âiné*, André Maurois and Villiers de l'Isle-Adam – each of whom wrote at least one sf piece – has been carried on in the work of Jean Hougren (*Le signe du chien*, 1961), Robert Merle (*Un animal doué de raison*, 1967; English title: *The Day of the Dolphin*) and Pierre Boulle (*The Planet of the Apes*, 1963). Edward de Capoulet-Junac's *Pallas ou la tribulation* (1967) – a book poorly received in

France – may well be the best novel of modern French sf, a caustic commentary on mankind in general and the science fiction BEM story in particular.

George Méliès in his own film, The India Rubber Head.

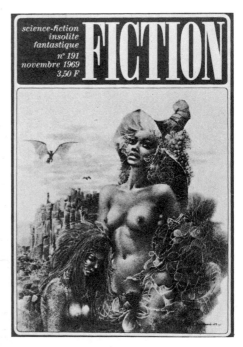

(*Opposite*) *Fiction based on fact: contemporary Japanese sf illustrations.*

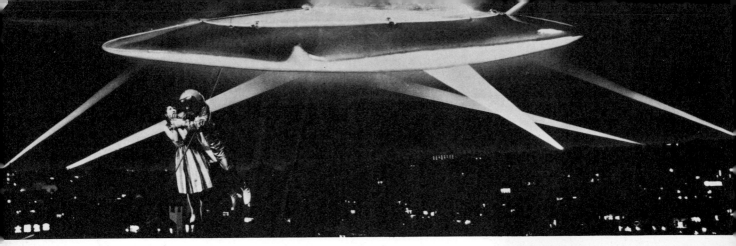

Opinion of Japanese sf has to a great extent been formed by a series of naive, though sometimes technically impressive, monster movies directed by Ishiro Honda. Starting with *Godzilla* (1955) and *Rodan* (1957), through *The Mysterians* (1957), a gallery of monsters with exotic names like Marjin, Gamera, Barugon or Ghidorah have fought mankind and each other, spectacularly wrecking cities and doing mischief in the country.

The emergence of these hypertrophic beasts is more often than not attributed to atomic tests. But once lip-service has been paid to a protest against the misuse of nuclear power, the proper business of these films can begin: the extermination contest fought with claws, fangs and beaks.

Just as in other countries, however, 'sf' films and written sf are two separate things, the latter being of a much higher standard. After World War II, Japan developed a remarkably large and varied science fiction field. One publisher alone, Hayakawa-shobo, besides publishing a sf magazine with a circulation of some 80,000 copies, has issued more than 300 science fiction books, mostly translations of Anglo-Saxon authors, but including also European writers as well as original Japanese books. In classic Japanese literature, both Ryunosuke Akutawaga (author of *Rashomon*, 1892–1927) and Edowaga Rampo (1894–1965) wrote fantastic tales, and this tradition is being continued today by the remarkable Kobo Abé (1924–   ), winner of the most important Japanese literary prize, the Akutawaga, in 1951. He has made a few journeys into the country of true sf, the most important being his novel

Dai Yon Kampyo-ki (1959) or *Inter Ice-Age 4*. Written in a lean, precise prose, this novel offers a glimpse into a bleak future when the polar ice caps begin to melt, and a group of human beings is remaking man into 'aquans' to adapt him to an underwater existence. Abé views these experiments, while admitting their necessity, with a critical eye, and is shocked by their ruthlessness. Superficially a mystery novel, the book poses serious moral dilemmas, showing liberty and free will at odds with necessity. The conflict between the hero of the book, Prof. Katsumi, and the computer created by him for predicting the future, provides the story with most of its tension, and is an ingenious and original variation on the *doppelgänger* motif.

A more ordinary kind of science fiction is written by the prolific Sakyo Komatsu (1931–   ), whose novel *Robbers of the Future* has been translated into several foreign languages. His *Nippon Chiubotsu* (*Submersible Japan*) sold more than one million copies in Japan and was made into a successful film. Other names in contemporary Japanese sf are Shin-Ichi Hoshi, Yasutaka Tsutsui, Ryu Misuse, Kazumasa Hirai, Fuzio Isihara or Aritsune Toyoda. Japanese sf fans are organized in 60 or 70 clubs. The SF Symposium in Osaka, in 1970, paralleling the World Fair, helped to bring Japanese science fiction to an international readership.

Japanese sf films: (*top*) The Mysterians, (*right*) *Godzilla and Rodan – potential destroyers of modern cities.* (*Opposite*) *Two illustrations from Kobo Abé's* Inter Ice-Age 4, *and* (*below*) *the hero in a Japanese sf film.*

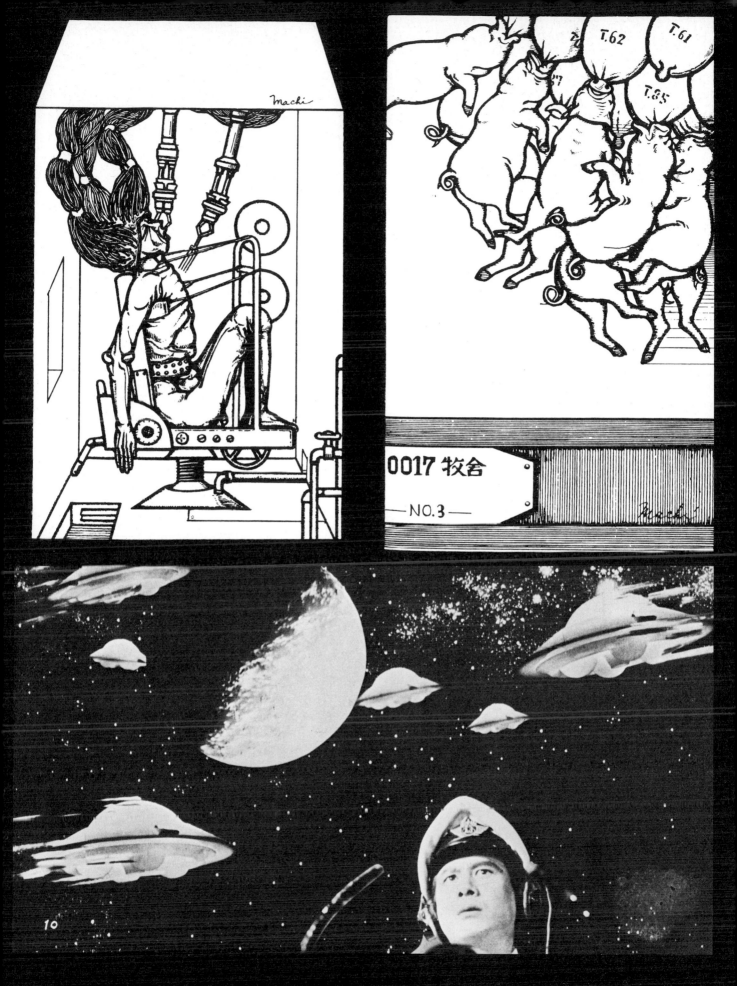

Italy, Spain, Rumania . . .

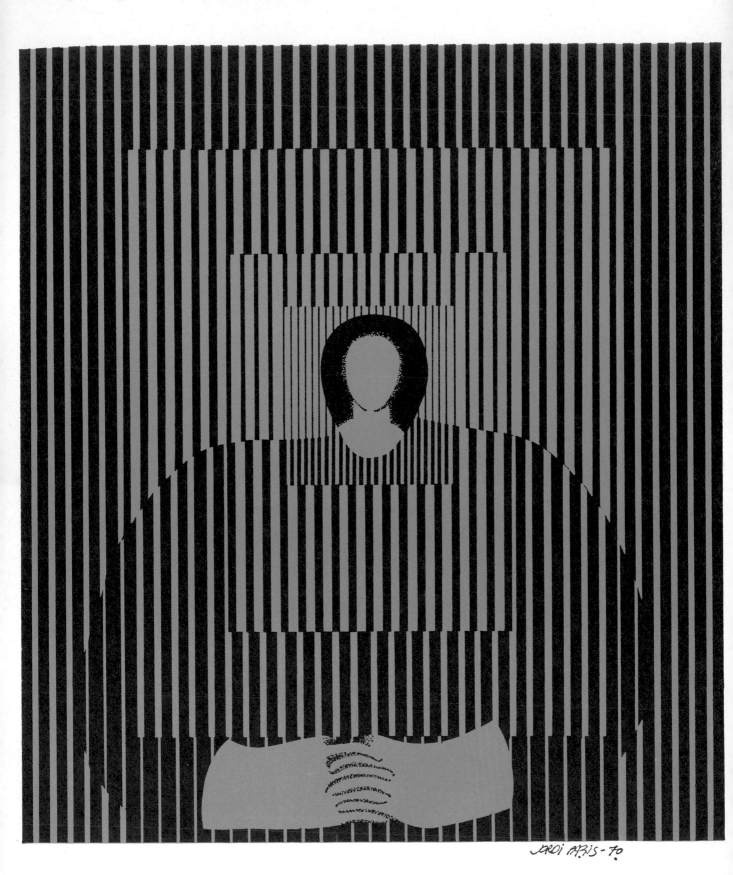

In Italy, Spain and Rumania, and also Germany, the situation of science fiction is similar: none of these countries has yet produced a really outstanding sf writer, although there are some promising ones. The stories that appear in those languages are often old-fashioned, sometimes well-written in a poetic language (such as those by Rumania's Vladimir Colin) but not very original. Science fiction magazines exist in all three countries. The Rumanian *Colectia Povestiri Stiintifico-Fantastice*, a modest bi-weekly publication, is the oldest, appearing since 1955; in Spain there is the well-produced and quite international *Nueva Dimension*, a magazine that competes with the Hungarian *Galaktika* for the title of the best-designed in the world; Italy can boast of several publications, of which the irregular *Nova SF*, edited by Ugo Malaguti, and *Gamma* are true sf magazines, while *Galassia* and Mondadori's *I Romanzi di Urania* are more like pocketbooks, featuring a novel or short-story collection in each issue. Many other Italian sf magazines, some of them reprints of U.S. magazines, have come and gone, with titles like *Cronache del Futuro*, *Alfa-Tauri*, *Cosmos* or *Futuria*. The cover art of many Italian sf magazines is of an extraordinarily high quality. *Galassia* regularly reproduces on its covers the work of respectable Italian artists, and *Urania* features the work of Karel Thole, a Dutchman living in Italy, whose work has also appeared on many American covers.

Only Rumania has developed a fairly large field of national writers, among whom Vladimir Colin, Adrian Rogoz and Sergiu Farcasan stand out; Italian and Spanish sf is largely dominated by Anglo-Saxon writers, with a number of younger authors, such as Ugo Malaguti, Gianni Montanari and Vittorio Curtoni, slowly making their way. More remarkable work has been done by respected contemporary Italian writers, especially Dino Buzzati (1906–72) and Italo Calvino (1923–). Buzzati has written a large number of very short, ironic horror-stories that start with a precise description of our world, exactly fixed in time and space, that slowly deteriorates and divulges a hidden horrible reality behind reality. Calvino's prose, in books like *Ti con zero* (1967, *t zero* in English) and *Le cosmicomiche* (1965, *Cosmicomics*) has more in common with Kafka and Raymond Queneau than with science fiction. These are *contes philosophiques*, highly abstract and intellectual, explicating in lean, concise narrative scientific and mathematical theorems, as in the tales of the space traveler '*Q fwfq*'.

Italian, Spanish and Rumanian sf illustration is of a high and exciting standard.

and Germany

The contemporary German sf scene, in the number of titles published annually, is second only to the U.S.A., but it is characterized by an almost total absence of original German-language sf of any worth. What little gets written by German authors is mostly destined to appear in cheap dime novels. Perry Rhodan, one of these series, has achieved a curious international success. Conceived by Clark Darlton (pseudonym for Walter Ernsting) and K. H. Scheer, the first issue of 'Perry Rhodan' appeared in 1961. Since then, nearly 600 novels have appeared in this weekly series, written by a team of authors, and selling close to 100 million copies, with translations into Japanese, Dutch, French and English. Getting its start with the first flight to the moon, the series has branched out into our galaxy and others, incorporating any theme or topic that was ever featured in science fiction. Long since immortalized to keep the series going, Galactic Administrator Perry Rhodan has averted countless dangers from the united world of mankind, battling the most fearful fiends. Crudely written, the Perry Rhodan books form a super-galactic space opera of all previous space operas rolled into one.

With no sf magazines to serve as a proving ground for aspiring young authors, a German sf author has either to opt for the little-esteemed dime novel series, or to try to get published by respectable book publishers. Only one writer has produced science fiction regularly over a number of years and of a quality that can be compared with the better international work: Viennese physicist Herbert W. Franke. When editor of the Goldmann sf series,

started in 1960, he wrote *The Green Comet* (1960), a volume of some 60 short-short stories, which, although relying heavily on surprise endings, showed the promise of a genuine talent, amply fulfilled later by his novels *The Thought Net* (1961), *Cage of Orchids* (1961), *The Desert of Steel* (1962), *The Glass Trap* (1962) and *Zone Null* (1970). Though over-involved, and with one-dimensional characters, they have nevertheless succeeded in evoking bleak portraits of future worlds controlled and manipulated by technocrats. Well-grounded in the sciences, these novels incorporate urgent problems of actual future possibilities. Being foremost a scientist, however, Franke is more interested in the things he wants to communicate than in the means of communicating them, and this makes his prose more notable for technical precision than for rhythm or wealth and depth of images. Ugly, joyless and structurally shapeless, his novels nevertheless convey a sense of desperation, presenting one scientific hell after another, with little hope for human freedom.

Illustration from the German sf magazine Utopia *(No. 2) for a van Vogt story. (Bottom) Diagram of Perry Rhodan's space ship.*

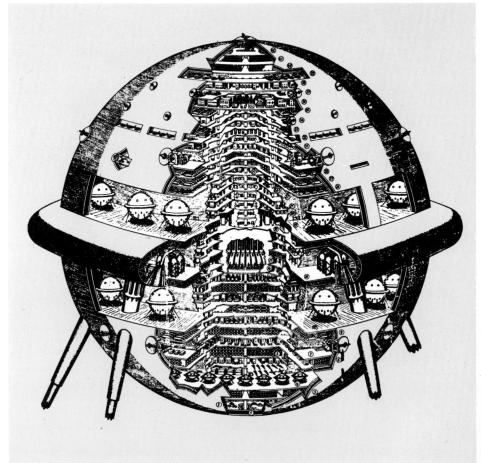

A joyfully mad cosmos: Kurt Vonnegut, Jr

In the course of twenty years Vonnegut has become one of America's best-known novelists and a spokesman of youth, despite his definitely middle-class attitudes. Beginning humbly with a fairly conventional dystopian science fiction novel, *Player Piano* (1952), while in the employ of General Electrics, through slick commercial short stories for the magazines, he hit his stride with idiosyncratic and irreverent sf novels like *The Sirens of Titan* (1959), *Cat's Cradle* (1963), *God Bless You, Mr. Rosewater* (1965) and *Slaughterhouse Five* (1969). His work, baffling and incongruous, inexplicable and infuriating, is full of 'chrono-synclastic infundibulums', time-travelling robots from mysterious Trafalmadore, mad scientists, even madder founders of religions, sf concepts like Ice-Nine and doomsday machines, and caricatures of the contemporary scene. Written with verve and gusto, with a keen sense for the ludicrous, in short, hectic sentences, arranged in equally short chapters for busy people who have time only to read a few chapters at a time, Vonnegut's outrageously preposterous, wildly comic and funny novels take the reader on a tour through a roller-coaster universe. Achieving fame late in his career, after many years as a neglected paperback writer, Vonnegut has remained a controversial figure, in science fiction and in the larger world. For Leslie Fiedler, Vonnegut's science fiction represents 'a way of releasing his own sentimental-ironic view of a meaningless universe redeemed by love'; for Charles Thomas Samuels, on the other hand (writing in *The New Republic*, June 12, 1971), Vonnegut 'can tell us nothing worth knowing except what his rise itself indicates: ours is an age in which adolescent ridicule can become a mode of upward mobility.' In sf circles, Vonnegut is often thought of as a renegade, having dared to criticize sf.

Deeply formed by the traumas of the fire-bombing of Dresden that Vonnegut experienced as a German prisoner of war, and Hiroshima, distrustful of science as a saving power ('What actually happened was that we dropped scientific truth on Hiroshima'), his work is a cheerful, respectlessly parodistic and satiric attempt to come to grips with a meaningless universe that offers nothing but a series of small and large apocalypses, with man thrown around by the forces of time, space and society, powerless to control his own destiny or indeed to change anything. Fiction cannot present any truths, because there aren't any; what the writer can do is to provide useful and comforting lies. 'When a man becomes a writer . . . he takes on a sacred obligation to produce beauty and enlightenment at top speed' (*Cat's Cradle*). The first sentence in 'The Book of Bokonon', the holy book of the fictitious religion in *Cat's Cradle*, boldly declares: 'All the true things I am about to tell you are shameless lies.'

A still from the film production of Kurt Vonnegut, Jr's Slaughterhouse Five.

Stanisław Lem, the greatest contemporary sf writer

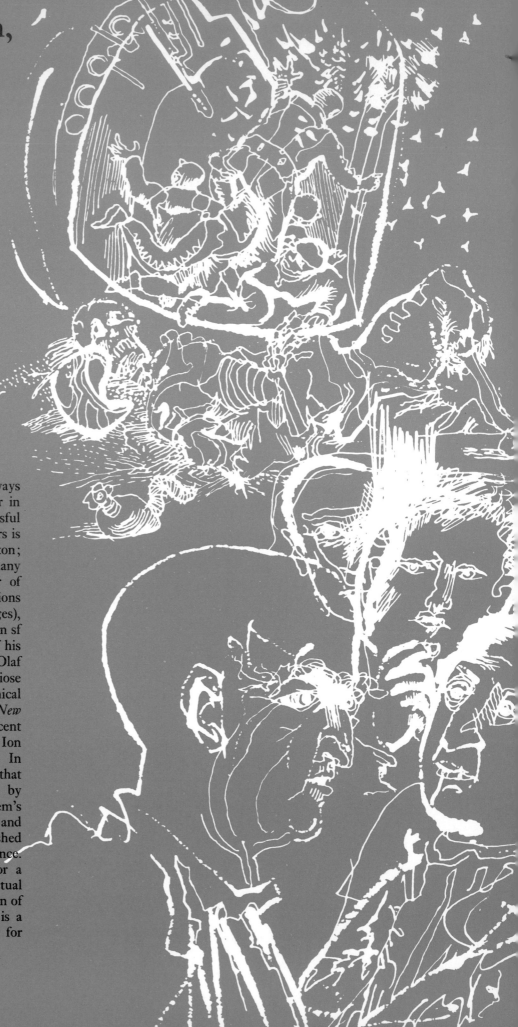

Although science fiction has always been most productive and popular in the United States, the most successful and best known of today's sf writers is neither an American nor a Briton; oddly enough, he is a Pole. In many ways, Stanisław Lem, the author of some thirty books (with translations into about twenty-eight languages), is the closest to H. G. Wells modern sf has yet produced; other aspects of his work betray an affinity with Olaf Stapledon, particularly the grandiose concepts developed in philosophical stories such as *Solaris* or *The New Cosmogony*; still others are reminiscent of Borges and Čapek (as in Lem's Ion Tichy and 'robot fables' cycles). In fact, the reader might suspect that these stories had been written by entirely different men. But all Lem's works, however varied in style and approach they may be, are distinguished by a serious attitude toward science. Neither a superficial optimist nor a fashionable pessimist, his intellectual approach is one relevant to a 'fiction of science': always questioning, his is a critical mind which takes nothing for granted.

(*Opposite*) *Illustration by Hegedüs István to one of Lem's books.*

Lem's most famous sf novel is perhaps *Solaris* (1961) which reads, according to one British reviewer, like an 'inspired collaboration between Freud and H. G. Wells.' His strength is bold speculation on almost any subject from information theory and cybernetics to linguistics, the philosophy of science, and cultural analysis. He has also won international recognition for his philosophical work, especially his attempt at a 'sociology of extraterrestrial civilizations.' One such paper was included in a scientific symposium published by the Soviet Academy of Sciences in 1972. Lem's best-known books include *The Astronauts* (1951), *The Invincible* (1963), *The Cyberiad* (1965), *Memoirs Found in a Bathtub* (1961) and *Tales of Pirx the Pilot*. Many of his stories have been turned into movies or television plays. Born in Lemberg in 1921 and originally trained as a physician, Lem has been residing in Cracow since 1945.

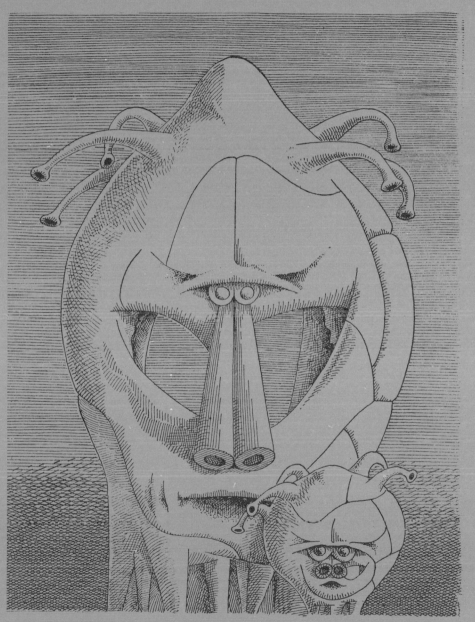

STANISŁAW LEM
INWAZJA z ALDEBARANA

Some other sf authors

A professor at Johns Hopkins University, China expert and pundit in psychological warfare wrote some of the strangest science fiction stories ever created: Paul Myron Anthony Linebarger (1913–66), who used the pseudonym Cordwainer Smith. Unlike the vaudeville banalizations of myth that are fashionable in much of current pulp sf, Cordwainer Smith's legends from a future world of 15,000 AD possess genuine mythic qualities, treating their subjects with respect and compassion, and adapting grand themes from our rich literary heritage in a future setting that is familiar and utterly strange at the same time. Smith's is a universe of grandiose and glorious deeds, peopled with space pilots and habermans, 'pinlighters' and 'underpeople,' animal-people endowed with intelligence. Most of the wealth of mankind is concentrated on the planet Norstrilia, a utopia of a simple and vigorous life, where the immortality drug Stroon is produced. Presenting a universe of traditional values, an aristocracy of the spirit, these tales tell of superhuman feats, curious human-animal relationships, and loves that conquer even the boundaries of time and space. The mass of humanity lead contented lives, cared for and watched over by a few responsible doers, the Lords and Ladies of the Instrumentality, rulers of all mankind. It is a universe of stark and violent feelings, where man's humanity is measured by his ability and willingness to suffer pain, bear responsibility and resist the allure of the easy life. It is this quality that makes Smith's under-people, particularly the girly-girl C'Mell (C for cat) and the new Johanna D'Joan (D for dog) so much more human than the majority of the true humans, who don't really live.

Cyclical narratives, interwoven, inconsistent and sometimes contradictory like historically grown myths, Cordwainer Smith's tales, written in evocative images and an almost incantory, ritual language, present not some pseudo-factual account of the future, but convey an outlook, a world-view, colored and distorted as if transmitted by oral tradition, and undoubtedly formed by the periods of the author's illnesses.

In *The Left Hand of Darkness* (1969) Ursula K. Le Guin, a remarkably sane and cultured writer, winner of a National Book Award for children's books, has painstakingly detailed another world, in which the inhabitants' sex is not fixed but variable, adding a new dimension of uncertainty to life. Her ability to create whole worlds is best employed, though, in a trilogy of beautifully written fantasies, *A Wizard of Earthsea* (1968), *The Tombs of Atuan* (1971) and *The Farthest Shore* (1972).

Of the *Galaxy* school of writers of the 'fifties, who relied more on sociological extrapolation and slick writing than technology (its best-known example is probably the satire on Madison Avenue *Gravy Planet* or *The Space Merchants* by the writing team of Frederik Pohl and C. M. Kornbluth), the most prominent may be Robert Sheckley. Although many of his short stories are one-punchers, simplicist tales aiming at surprising the reader by a paradoxical ending, he has written a fair number of wildly funny and inventive journeys through possible and impossible, mostly mad worlds, that are somewhat akin to the works of Kurt Vonnegut, Jr, although of a lesser order. The novels *Immortality, Inc.* (1959), *Mindswap* (1966) and *Dimension of Miracles* (1968) are good examples of his sharp wit, but he is at his best in satirical short stories like 'Love, Inc.'

Philip K. Dick may not be so successful as Vonnegut but he is possibly a more substantial writer. Obviously there exist certain similarities between the work of the two men, in that both make use of the fantastic imagery supplied by sf to treat much more serious metaphysical questions. Dick's psychotic and tormenting worlds, in books like *The Three Stigmata of Palmer Eldritch* (1964) or *Ubik* (1969), dissolve our familiar concepts of cause and effect, distort our perception of time and space, and turn the universe into a sinister, hellish place, where a façade of reality forms a thin layer over a seething chaos.

Much of Dick's work is of an inferior quality, but in his best novels he becomes an existentialist sf writer of considerable impact.

'A Planet Named Shagol,' by Cordwainer Smith, illustrated by Virgil Finlay (Galaxy, October 1961).

Sf fandom

'Fiawol'; 'Gafia'; 'Fijagh.' Do these names ring a bell with you? How about 'fanac', 'prodom', 'ayjay', 'fringefans'? No? Then you aren't a bnf ('big name fan,' i.e., a well-known fan) or a 'trufan' (real fan), and perhaps you're no science fiction fan at all. These are only a few examples from the slang developed by 'fandom', the community of science fiction aficionados. Translated into plain English, they mean:

Gafia – getting away from it all; becoming inactive in fandom.

Fiawol – fandom is a way of life; as opposed to:

Fijagh – fandom is just a goddamn hobby.

fanac – fan activity; everything connected with sf as a hobby, such as writing letters, publishing fanzines (the amateur magazines of sf) or attending Cons (sf conventions).

prodom – professionals 'as a subdivision of humanity; all the people earning money from writing, editing, agenting or publishing science fiction.'

ayjay – amateur journalism.

fringefan – someone who is barely a fan.

These expressions and many more are fully explained in Harry Warner, Jr's *All Our Yesterdays*, a 'history of fandom in the 'forties' (New York, 1971).

The vociferous lobby of sf readers, and the close contact between sf writers and readers, are unparalleled in any other kind of fiction, popular or highbrow. It is a phenomenon that goes back to the founding of *Amazing Stories* in 1926, for the sf magazine made possible what the dime novel could not do: the readers' columns served as a central sounding board for enthusiasts, who soon began to exchange letters among themselves. Clubs – first devoted to discussions of science, then to discussions of sf – sprang into existence, and the amateur magazines known as 'fanzines' began to appear. In May 1930, members of the 'Science Correspondence Club' issued a newsletter, *The Comet* (later retitled *Cosmology*); other legendary fanzines were *The Time Traveler*, *Science Fiction Digest* and *Fantasy Man*. Many early fans went on to become professional writers, editors and artists; the list includes Julius Schwartz, Mortimer Weisinger, Damon Knight, Frederik Pohl, Donald A. Wollheim, and James Blish. Arthur C. Clarke and Ray Bradbury got their start writing for fanzines as well, and Bradbury published his own fanzine, *Futuria Fantasia*, in 1939. One fan, seventeen-year-old Charles D. Hornig, was hired by Hugo Gernsback as editor of *Wonder Stories* on the strength of the first issue of his fanzine *Fantasy Fan*.

Hundreds of fanzines have come and gone since then, with circulations ranging from a few copies to 1500. Today they are published in almost all countries with a fair-sized sf publishing market, even behind the Iron Curtain. An entire book has been devoted to their history (*The World of Fanzines*, by Fredric Wertham, 1973).

A further focal point in the social life of sf aficionados is the schedule of regional, national or international science fiction conventions or 'Cons,' where fans and pros meet, make speeches, discuss problems, or just plain gossip. The first World Science Fiction Convention was held in New York on July 4, 1939; since then, world cons and smaller conventions have been held regularly, except for a brief interlude during World War II, and every year there are dozens of them. At the Eleventh World Con (in Philadelphia in 1953) the first sf achievement awards – called 'Hugos' in honor of Gernsback – were presented, and soon became an annual event. Other notable 'fannish' institutions include TAFF, the Transatlantic Fan Fund, founded to bring an American fan to European conventions or make it possible for a European winner to visit the U.S.

Strangest of all, perhaps, is the existence of books like Sam Moskowitz's *The Immortal Storm* (1954), which chronicles the history of the feuds of a small segment of fandom with the detailed grandeur worthy of a history of empires. Whether fandom has done sf more good than harm is open to debate: while it has provided authors with a unique link to readers, the ghetto-like standards of sf criticism often act as a block to change, since fans tend to clamor for more of what they like. But few of those who have participated in fandom would deny that it is a wonderful experience, often more marvelous than much that is presented in sf itself.

Chronology of science fiction

The following list is a compromise between historically important literary works of science fiction, and works that are merely popular or influential. No individual short stories after 1931 have been listed, and only two representative sf anthologies of the many published are given here.

c. 160 LUCIAN *Vera Historia Icaromenippos*

1516 THOMAS MORUS *De optimo rei publicae statu deque nova insula Utopia*

1623 TOMMASO CAMPANELLA *Civitas solis*

1627 FRANCIS BACON *Nova Atlantis*

1634 JOHANN KEPLER *Somnium*

1638 FRANCIS GODWIN *The Man in the Moone*
JOHN WILKINS *A Discourse Concerning a New World and Another Planet*

1650 CYRANO DE BERGERAC *L'autre monde ou les états et empires de la lune*

1662 CYRANO DE BERGERAC *Histoire comique des états et empires du soleil*

1656 JAMES HARRINGTON *Oceana*

1726 JONATHAN SWIFT *Travels into Several Remote Nations of the World, by Lemuel G.*

1727 SAMUEL BRUNT *A Voyage to Cacklogallinia*

1741 LUDVIG HOLBERG *Journey of Niels Klim Underground (Nicolai Klimii iter subterraneum)*

1744 EBERHARD CHRISTIAN KINDERMANN *Swift Journey by Air-Ship to the Upper World (Geschwinde Reise auf dem Luftschiff nach der oberen Welt)*

1751 ROBERT PALTOCK *The Life and Adventures of Peter Wilkins*

1752 VOLTAIRE *Micromégas*

1763 ANONYMOUS 'The Reign of George VI, 1900–1925'

1771 LOUIS SEBASTIEN MERCIER *The Year 2440 (L'an 2440, ou rêve s'il en fut jamais)*

1781 RESTIF DE LA BRETONNE *The Flying Man (La découverte australe par un homme volant, ou Le Dédale français)*

1785 WILHELM FRIEDRICH VON MEYERN *Dya-Na-Sore, oder die Wanderer*

1788 GIACOMO CASANOVA *L'Icosameron*

1790 CARL IGNAZ GEIGER *Journey of an Earthman to Mars*

1810 JULIUS VON VOSS *Ini. Ein Roman aus dem einundzwanzigsten Jahrhundert*

1817 MARY SHELLEY *Frankenstein, or the Modern Prometheus*

1826 MARY SHELLEY *The Last Man*

1829 E. A. POE *Tales of the Grotesque and Arabesque*

1842 ETIENNE CABET *Voyage to Icarie*

1858 FITZ-JAMES O'BRIEN 'The Diamond Lens'

1862 N. G. CHERNYSHEVSKY *What Is To be Done? (Chto delat'?)*

1864 JULES VERNE *Journey to the Center of the Earth (Voyage au centre de la terre)*

1865 JULES VERNE *Journey to the Moon (De la terre à la lune)*

1869 JULES VERNE *Twenty Thousand Leagues under the Sea (Vingt mille lieues sous la mer)*

1870 JULES VERNE *Journey around the Moon (Autour de la lune)*

1871 G. T. CHESNEY 'The Battle of Dorking. Reminiscences of a Volunteer'

1872 SAMUEL BUTLER *Erewhon or Over the Range*
MÓR JOKAI *The Novel of the Coming Century (A jövő százád regenye)*

1873 EDWARD BULWER LYTTON *The Coming Race*

1877 JULES VERNE *Off on a Comet (Hector Servadac)*

1878 KURD LASSWITZ *Pictures from the Future (Bilder aus der Zukunft)*

1880 PERCY GREGG *Across the Zodiac*

1882 ALBERT ROBIDA *The Twentieth Century (Le vingtième siècle)*

1883 ALBERT ROBIDA *The War of the Twentieth Century (La guerre au vingtième siècle)*

1886 VILLIERS DE L'ISLE-ADAM *The Eve of the Future (L'Eve future)*
ROBERT LOUIS STEVENSON *Strange Case of Dr Jekyll and Mr Hyde*

1887 J. H. ROSNY AÎNÉ 'Les Xipéhuz'

1888 EDWARD BELLAMY *Looking Backward 2000–1887*

1889 T. HERTZKA *A Journey to Freeland (Eine Reise nach Freiland)*
FRANK R. STOCKTON *The Great War Syndicate*
MARK TWAIN *A Connecticut Yankee in King Arthur's Court*

1890 IGNATIUS DONNELLY *Caesar's Column*

1891 WILLIAM MORRIS *News from Nowhere*

1895 K. E. TSIOLKOVSKY 'Dreams of Earth and the Sky' ('Grezy o zemle i nebe')

H. G. WELLS *The Time Machine*

1896 H. G. WELLS *The Island of Dr Moreau*

H. G. WELLS *The Invisible Man*

1897 KURD LASSWITZ *Two Planets (Auf zwei Planeten)*

1898 H. G. WELLS *The War of the Worlds*
M. P. SHIEL *The Yellow Danger*

1899 H. G. WELLS *Tales of Space and Time*

1900 THEODOR HERZL *Old Newland (Altneuland)*

1901 M. P. SHIEL *The Lord of the Sea*
M. P. SHIEL *The Purple Cloud*
H. G. WELLS *The First Men in the Moon*

1903 JERZY ZUŁAWSKI *The Silver Globe (Na srebrnym globie)*

1904 G. K. CHESTERTON *The Napoleon of Notting Hill*

1907 R. H. BENSON *The Lord of the World*
JACK LONDON *The Iron Heel*

1908 ANATOLE FRANCE *Penguin Island (L'île des pingouins)*

1909 RUDYARD KIPLING 'With the Night Mail'
AMBROSE BIERCE 'Moxon's Master'

1911 HUGO GERNSBACK *Ralph 124 C 41+*
J. D. BERESFORD *The Hampdenshire Wonder*
G. P. SERVISS *A Columbus of Space*

1912 EDGAR RICE BURROUGHS *Under the Moons of Mars (A Princess of Mars)*
E. M. FORSTER 'The Machine Stops'
ARTHUR CONAN DOYLE *The Lost World*
WILLIAM HOPE HODGSON *The Nightland*
J. H. ROSNY AÎNÉ 'The Death of Earth' ('Le mort de la terre')

1913 PAUL SCHEERBART *Lesabèndio*
BERNHARD KELLERMANN *The Tunnel (Der Tunnel)*

1918 VLADIMIR MAYAKOVSKY *Mystery-Bouffe (Misteriia Buff)*

1920 KAREL ČAPEK *R.U.R.*
EVGENY ZAMYATIN *We (My, published in 1922 in Paris)*

1922 ALEXEI TOLSTOY *Aelita*

1924 ILYA EHRENBURG *Trust DE (Trest DE)*
ALFRED DÖBLIN *Giants (Giganten)*

1925 SYDNEY FOWLER WRIGHT *The Amphibians*

1928 E. E. SMITH *The Skylark of Space*
ANDRÉ MAUROIS 'The War

Against the Moon' ('*Fragments d'une histoire universelle*')

1930 OLAF STAPLEDON *Last and First Men*

1931 JOHN TAINE *The Time Stream*
ANDRÉ MAUROIS 'The Weigher of Souls' ('*Le Peseur d'âmes*')

1932 ALDOUS HUXLEY *Brave New World*

1934 JOHN TAINE *Before the Dawn*

1935 OLAF STAPLEDON *Odd John*

1936 KAREL ČAPEK *War with the Newts* (*Valka s mloky*)

1937 OLAF STAPLEDON *Star Maker*

1938 C. S. LEWIS *Out of the Silent Planet*

1939–50, 1973 ROBERT A. HEINLEIN *The History of the Future* series

1940 A. E. VAN VOGT *Slan*

1942–9 ISAAC ASIMOV *Foundation* series

1943 C. S. LEWIS *Perelandra*

1944 OLAF STAPLEDON *Sirius*

1945 C. S. LEWIS *That Hideous Strength*

1945 A. E. VAN VOGT *The World of Null-A*

1946 GROFF CONKLIN, ED. *The Best of Science Fiction*
RAYMOND J. HEALY AND J. FRANCIS McCOMAS, ED. *Adventures in Time and Space*

1949 GEORGE ORWELL *1984*
GEORGE R. STEWART *Earth Abides*

1950 ISAAC ASIMOV *I, Robot*
RAY BRADBURY *The Martian Chronicles*
A. E. VAN VOGT *The Voyage of the Space Beagle*

1951 RAY BRADBURY *The Illustrated Man*

1952 CLIFFORD D. SIMAK *City*

1953 ALFRED BESTER *The Demolished Man*
ARTHUR C. CLARKE *Childhood's End*
THEODORE STURGEON *More Than Human*
FREDERIK POHL AND C. M. KORNBLUTH *The Space Merchants*

1955 JAMES BLISH *Earthman, Come Home*

1956 ALFRED BESTER *The Stars My Destination*

1957 STANISLAW LEM *Star Diaries* (*Dzienniki gwiazdowe*)

1957–8 IVAN EFREMOV *The Andromeda Nebula* (*Tumannost' Andromedy*)

1958 JAMES BLISH *A Case of Conscience*

1959 WALTER M. MILLER, JR. *A Canticle for Leibowitz*
KURT VONNEGUT, JR. *The Sirens of Titan*
KOBO ABÉ *Inter Ice-Age 4* (*Dai Yon Kampyo-ki*)

1961 HERBERT W. FRANKE *The Orchid Cage* (*Der Orchideenkäfig*)
ROBERT A. HEINLEIN *Stranger in a Strange Land*
JEAN HOUGREN *The Sign of the Dog* (*Le Signe du Chien*)
STANISŁAW LEM *Solaris*

1963 KURT VONNEGUT, JR *Cat's Cradle*

1964 PHILIP K. DICK *The Three Stigmata of Palmer Eldritch*
ARKADI AND BORIS STRUGATSKI *Hard To Be a God* (*Trudno byt' bogom*)

1965 FRANK HERBERT *Dune*
CORDWAINER SMITH *Space Lords*
STANISŁAW LEM *The Cyberiad* (*Cyberiada*)

1965–6 ARKADI AND BORIS STRUGATSKI *The Snail on the Slope* (*Ulitka na sklone*)

1966 J. G. BALLARD *The Crystal World*

1967 ARKADI AND BORIS STRUGATSKI *The Fairytale of the Troika* (*Skazka o troike*)

1968 THOMAS M. DISCH *Camp Concentration*
STANISŁAW LEM *His Master's Voice* (*Głos Pana*)

1969 BRIAN W. ALDISS *Barefoot in the Head*
PHILIP K. DICK *Ubik*
URSULA K. LE GUIN *The Left Hand of Darkness*

1969 KURT VONNEGUT, JR *Slaughterhouse Five*

1970 HERBERT W. FRANKE *Zone Null*

1974 URSULA K. LE GUIN *The Dispossessed*

SELECT BIBLIOGRAPHY
Reference works

BERTONI, ALFIO and GIANLUIGI MISSIAJA *Catalogo Generale della Fantascienza.* Venezia: Edizioni Centro Cultori Science Fiction, 1968.

BIESTERFELD, WOLFGANG *Die literarische Utopie.* Stuttgart: J. B. Metzlersche Verlagsbuchhandlung, 1974.

BINGENHEIMER, HEINZ *Transgalaxis. Katalog der deutschsprachigen utopisch-phantastischen Literatur aus fünf Jahrhunderten* (*1460–1960*). Friedrichsdorf/Taunus: Transgalaxis, 1959/1960.

BLEILER, EVERETT F. *The Checklist of Fantastic Literature. A Bibliography of Fantasy, Weird, and Science Fiction Books Published in the English Language.* Chicago: Shasta Publishers, 1948.

BLEYMEHL, JAKOB *Beiträge zur Geschichte und Bibliographie der utopischen und phantastischen Literatur.* Fürth/Saar: Jakob Bleymehl, 1965.

BRINEY, ROBERT E. and EDWARD WOOD *SF Bibliographies. An Annotated Bibliography of Bibliographical Works on Science Fiction and Fantasy Fiction.* Chicago: Advent Publishers, 1972.

CLARESON, THOMAS D. *Science Fiction Criticism: An Annotated Checklist.* Kent (Ohio): Kent State University Press, 1972.

CLARKE, I. F. *The Tale of the Future.* London: The Library Association, 1961; 2nd edition, 1972.

COLE, WALTER R. *A Checklist of Science Fiction Anthologies.* Brooklyn: W. R. Cole, 1964.

DAY, BRADFORD M. *The Checklist of Fantastic Literature in Paperbound Books.* Denver: Science-Fiction and Fantasy Publications, 1965.

DAY, BRADFORD M. *An Index on the Weird and Fantastic in Magazines.* S. Ozone Park: Bradford M. Day, 1953.

DAY, BRADFORD M. *The Supplemental Checklist of Fantastic Literature.* Denver (New York): Science-Fiction and Fantasy Publications, 1963.

DAY, DONALD B. *Index to the Science-Fiction Magazines, 1926–50.* Portland (Oregon): Perri Press, 1952.

ELLIK, RON and BILL EVANS *The Universes of E. E. Smith.* Chicago: Advent Publishers, 1966.

FALKE, RITA 'Versuch einer Bibliographie der Utopien.' In *Romanistisches Jahrbuch 6* (1953–54), pp. 92–109.

GOVE, PHILIP BABCOCK *The Imaginary Voyage in Prose Fiction. A History of its Criticism and a Guide for its Study, with an Annotated Checklist of 215 Imaginary Voyages from 1700 to 1800.* London: Holland Press, 1961.

HEINS, HENRY HARDY *A Golden Anniversary Bibliography of Edgar Rice Burroughs.* West Kingston: Donald M. Grant, 1964.

Index to the Science Fiction Magazines 1966–70. Cambridge (Mass.): New England Science Fiction Association, 1971.

LEE, WALT *Reference Guide to Fantastic Films, Science Fiction, Fantasy, and Horror.* Los Angeles: Chelsea-Lee Books. Volume 1, A–F, 1972; Volume 2, G–O, 1973; Volume 3, P–Z, 1974.

LIAPUNOV, BORIS 'Bibliografiia.' In Britikov, A.: *Russkii sovetskii nauchno-fantasticheskii roman.* Leningrad: Izdatel'stvo 'Nauka,' 1970, pp. 363–436.

LIAPUNOV, BORIS *V mire mechty.* Moscow: Izdatel'stvo 'Kniga,' 1970

LUNDWALL, SAM J. *Bibliografi över Science Fiction och Fantasy.* Stockholm: Fiktiva, 1964.

METCALF, NORM *The Index of Science Fiction Magazines, 1951–65.* El Cerrito (Calif.): J. Ben Stark, 1968.

MILLER, MAJORIE M. *Isaac Asimov. A Checklist of Works Published in the United States, March 1939 – May 1972.* Kent: The Kent State University Press, 1972.

MORSE, A. REYNOLDS *The Works of M.P. Shiel.* Los Angeles: Fantasy Publishing Co., 1948.

OWINGS, MARK and JACK L. CHALKER *The Index to the Science-Fantasy Publishers.* Baltimore: The Anthem Series, 1966.

OWINGS, MARK and JACK L. CHALKER *The Revised H.P. Lovecraft Bibliography.* Baltimore: The Mirage Press, 1973.

REGINALD, ROBERT *STELLA NOVA: The Contemporary Science Fiction Authors.* Los Angeles: Unicorn & Son, 1970.

SIEMON, FREDERICK *Science Fiction Story Index 1950–68.* Chicago: American Library Association, 1971.

SUVIN, DARKO *Russian Science Fiction Literature and Criticism 1956–1970. A Bibliography.* Montreal: Secondary Universe 4 Conference, 1971.

SWIGART, LESLIE KAY *Harlan Ellison: A Bibliographical Checklist.* Los Angeles: Leslie Kay Swigart, 1973.

STONE, GRAHAM *Australian Science Fiction Index, 1925–67.* Canberra: Australian Science Fiction Association, 1968.

STRAUSS, ERWIN S. *The MIT Science Fiction Society's Index to the SF Magazines, 1951–65.* Cambridge (Mass.): MIT Science Fiction Society, 1966.

TUCK, DONALD H. *The Encyclopedia of Science Fiction and Fantasy.* Chicago: Advent Publishers. Volume 1: Who's Who, A–L. 1974. (Vols. 2 and 3 will appear in 1976 and 1977 respectively.)

TUCK, DONALD H. *A Handbook of Science Fiction and Fantasy* (2nd edition). Hobart (Tasmania): Donald H. Tuck, 1959.

Utopisztikus Tudományos Fantasztikus Müvek. Bibliográfiája. Miskolc, 1970.

VERSINS, PIERRE *Encyclopédie de l'utopie, des voyages extraordinaires et de la science fiction.* Lausanne: L'Age d' Homme, 1972.

WEST, RICHARD C. *Tolkien Criticism. An Annotated Checklist.* Kent: The Kent State University Press, 1970, 1972.

Books about science fiction and fantasy

AGEL, JEROME (ed.) *The Making of Kubrick's 2001.* New York: New American Library, 1970.

ALDANI, LINO *La Fantascienza.* Piacenza: Editrice La Tribuna, 1962.

ALDISS, BRIAN W. *Billion Year Spree. The history of science fiction.* London: Weidenfeld & Nicolson, 1973. New York: Doubleday & Co., 1973.

ALDISS, BRIAN W. *The Shape of Further Things. Speculations on change.* London: Faber and Faber, 1970.

AMIS, KINGSLEY *New Maps of Hell. A survey of Science Fiction.* New York: Harcourt Brace, 1960. London: Victor Gollancz Ltd., 1960.

APPEL, BENJAMIN *The Fantastic Mirror: Science Fiction Across the Ages.* New York: Random House, 1969.

ARMYTAGE, W. H. G. *Yesterday's Tomorrows. A historical survey of future societies.* London: Routledge & Kegan Paul, 1968.

ATHELING, WILLIAM, JR (JAMES BLISH) *The Issue at Hand. Studies in contemporary magazine Science Fiction.* Chicago: Advent Publishers, 1964.

ATHELING, WILLIAM, JR (JAMES BLISH) *More Issues at Hand. Critical studies in contemporary Science Fiction.* Chicago: Advent Publishers, 1972.

BAILEY, J. O. *Pilgrims Through Space and Time: Trends and Patterns in Scientific and Utopian Fiction.* New York: Argus Books, 1947. Westport: Greenwood Press, 1972.

BALCERZAK, EWA *Stanisław Lem.* Warsaw: Państwowy Instytut Wydawniczy, 1973.

BARMEYER, EIKE (ed.) *Science Fiction. Theorie und Geschichte.* Munich: Wilhelm Fink Verlag, 1972.

BAUDIN, HENRY *La Science-Fiction.* Paris-Montréal: Bordas, 1971.

BAXTER, JOHN *Science Fiction in the Cinema.* New York: A. S. Barnes & Co.; London: A. Zwemmer Limited, 1970.

BERGIER, JACQUES *Admirations.* Paris: Christian Bourgois, 1970.

BERGONZI, BERNARD *The Early H. G. Wells: A Study of the Scientific Romances.* Manchester: Manchester University Press, 1961.

BORN, FRANZ *Der Mann, der die Zukunft erfand.* Eupen: Markus Verlag, 1960.

BORRELLO, ALFRED *H. G. Wells, Author in Agony.* Carbondale and Edwardsville: Southern Illinois University Press, 1972.

BOUYXOU, J. P. *La science-fiction au cinéma.* Paris: Union Générale d'Editions, 1971.

BRANDIS, E. *Sovetskii nauchno-fantasticheskii roman.* Leningrad: Obch. po rasprostr. politch. i nauchn. Znanii, 1959.

BRANDIS, E. and V. DMITREVSKII *Cherez gory vremeni.* Moscow-Leningrad: Sovetski pisatel, 1963.

BRETNOR, REGINALD (ed.) *Modern Science Fiction: Its Meaning and Its Future.* New York: Coward-McCann, 1953.

BRETNOR, REGINALD (ed.) *Science Fiction, Today and Tomorrow.* New York: Harper and Row, 1974.

BRIDENNE, JEAN-JACQUES *La littérature française d'expression scientifique.* Paris: Dassonville, 1950.

BRITIKOV, A. *Russkii soveskii nauchno-fantaticheskii roman.* Leningrad: Izdatel'stvo 'Nauka,' 1970.

BROME, VINCENT *H. G. Wells. A biography.* London, New York, Toronto: Longmans, Green & Co., 1951.

BUCHNER, HERMANN *Programmiertes Glück. Sozialkritik in der utopischen Sowjetliteratur.* Wien, Frankfurt, Zürich: Europa Verlag, 1970.

BUTLER, IVAN *Horror in the Cinema.* London: A. Zwemmer Limited; New York: A. S. Barnes & Co., 1967.

CAILLOIS, ROGER *Images, images . . . Essais sur le rôle et les pouvoirs d l'imagination.* Paris: Librairie José Corti, 1966.

CANTRIL, HADLEY *The Invasion from Mars.* Princeton: Princeton University Press, 1952.

CARRELL, CHRISTOPHER (ed.) *Beyond This Horizon. An anthology of Science Fiction and science fact.* Sunderland: Ceolfrith Press, 1973.

CARTER, LIN *Imaginary Worlds. The art of fantasy.* New York: Ballantine Books, 1973.

CARTER, LIN *Lovecraft: A Look Behind the 'Chulhu Mythos.'* New York: Ballantine Books, 1972.

CARTER, LIN *Tolkien: A Look Behind the Lord of the Rings.* New York: Ballantine Books, 1969.

CHERNAYA, N. I. *V mire mechty i predvidenii.* Kiev: Naukova dumka, 1972.

CHESNEAUX, JEAN *The Political and Social Ideas of Jules Verne.* London: Thames & Hudson, 1972.

CLARENS, CARLOS *An Illustrated History of the Horror Film.* New York: Capricorn Books, 1967.

CLARESON, THOMAS D. (ed.) *SF: The Other Side of Realism. Essays on modern Fantasy and Science Fiction.* Bowling Green, Ohio: Bowling Green University Popular Press, 1971.

CLARKE, I. F. *Voices Prophesying War, 1763–1984.* New York and London: Oxford University Press, 1966.

COUPERIE, PIERRE and MAURICE C. HORN *A History of the Comic Strip.* New York: Crown Publishers, 1968.

DANIELS, LES *Comix. A History of Comic Books in America.* New York: Outerbridge & Dienstfrey, 1971.

DAVENPORT, BASIL *Inquiry Into Science Fiction.* New York: Longmans, Green, 1955.

DAVENPORT, BASIL (ed.) *The Science Fiction Novel: Imagination and Social Criticism.* Chicago: Advent Publishers, 1964.

DE CAMP, L. SPRAGUE (ed.) *The Conan Reader.* Baltimore: The Mirage Press, 1968.

DE CAMP, L. SPRAGUE (ed.) *The Conan Swordbook.* Baltimore: The Mirage Press, 1969.

DE CAMP, L. SPRAGUE *Science-Fiction Handbook: The Writing of Imaginative Fiction.* New York: Hermitage House, 1953.

DE CAMP, L. SPRAGUE and GEORGE H. SCITHERS (ed.) *The Conan Grimoire.* Baltimore: The Mirage Press, 1972.

DE DIESBACH, GHISLAIN *Le tour de Jules Verne en quatre-vingts livres.* Paris: Julliard, 1969.

DE LA FUYË, MARGUERITE *Jules Verne, sa vie – son oeuvre.* Paris: Hachette, 1953.

DIFFLOTH, GÉRARD *La science-fiction.* Paris: Gamma-Presse, 1964.

DUMONT, JEAN-PAUL and JEAN MONOD *Le Foetus Astral.* Paris: Christian Bourgois, 1970.

EIZYKMAN, BORIS *Science fiction et capitalisme. Critique de la position de désir de la science.* Paris: Maison Mame, 1973.

ELLIOTT, ROBERT C. *The Shape of Utopia: Studies in a Literary Genre.* Chicago: University of Chicago Press, 1970.

ELLWOOD, GRACIA FAY *Good News from Tolkien's Middle Earth.* Grand Rapids, Michigan: William B. Eerdmans Publishing Company, 1970.

ESCAICH, RENÉ *Voyage à travers le monde vernien.* Brussels: Edition La Boétie, 1951.

ESCAICH, RENÉ *Voyage au monde de Jules Verne.* Paris: Edit. Plantin, 1955.

ESHBACH, LLOYD ARTHUR *Of Worlds Beyond: The Science of Science Fiction Writing.* Reading: Fantasy Press, 1947. Chicago: Advent Publishers, 1964.

EVANS, ROBLEY *J. R. R. Tolkien.* New York: Warner Paperback Library, 1972.

FEIFFER, JULES *The Great Comic Book Heroes.* New York: Bonanza Books, 1965.

FERRINI, FRANCO *Che Cos E': La fantascienza.* Roma: Ubaldini Editore, 1970.

FRANK, BERNARD *Jules Verne et ses voyages.* Paris: Flammarion, 1941.

FRANKLIN, H. BRUCE *Future Perfect: American Science Fiction of the Nineteenth Century.* New York: Oxford University Press, 1966.

FUKUSHIMA, MASAMI (ed.) *SF Nyumon.* Tokyo: Hayakawa shobo, 1960.

FUKUSHIMA, MASAMI *SF Sanpo.* Tokyo: Bunsen, 1973.

FUKUSHIMA, MASAMI *SF No Me.* Tokyo: Tairin, 1973.

GATTEGNO, JEAN *La science-fiction.* Paris: Presses Universitaires de France, 'Que sais-je?', 1971.

GERBER, RICHARD *Utopian Fantasy: A Study of English Utopian Fiction Since the end of the Nineteenth Century.* London: Routledge & Kegan Paul, 1955. New York: McGraw-Hill, 1973.

GERROLD, DAVID *The World of Star Trek.* New York: Ballantine Books, 1973.

GIFFORD, DENIS *Movie Monsters.* London: Studio Vista, 1969.

GIFFORD, DENIS *Science Fiction Film.* London: Studio Vista, 1971.

GOODSTONE, TONY *The Pulps. Fifty years of American pop culture.* New York: Chelsea House, 1970.

GOULART, RON *An Informal History of the Pulp Magazines.* New York: Arlington House, 1972.

GRAAF, VERA *Homo Futurus. Eine Analyse der modernen Science Fiction.* Hamburg and Düsseldorf: Claassen Verlag, 1971.

GREEN, ROGER LANCELYN *Into Other Worlds: Space Flight in Fiction from Lucian to Lewis.* New York: Abelard-Schuman, 1958.

GÜNTHER, GOTTHARD *Die Entdeckung Amerikas und die Sache der Weltraumliteratur.* Düsseldorf: Karl Rauch Verlag, 1952.

GUREVICH, G. *Karta strany fantazii.* Moscow: Iskusstvo, 1967.

HANDKE, RYSZARD *Polska proza fantastyczno-naukowa. Problemy poetyki.* Wrocław-Warsaw-Kraków: Zakład narodowy imienia Ossolińskich Wydawnictwo Polskiej Akademii Nauk, 1969.

HASSELBLATT, DIETER *Die grünen Männchen vom Mars. Science Fiction für Leser und Macher.* Düsseldorf: Droste Verlag, 1974.

HAY, GEORGE (ed.) *The Disappearing Future. A symposium of speculation.* London: Panther Books, 1970.

HIENGER, JÖRG *Literarische Zukunftphantastik. Eine Studie über Science Fiction.* Göttingen: Vandenhoeck & Ruprecht, 1972.

HILLEGAS, MARK R. *The Future as Nightmare: H. G. Wells and the Anti-Utopians.* New York: Oxford University Press, 1967.

HILLEGAS, MARK R. (ed.) *Shadows of Imagination: The Fantasies of C. S. Lewis, J. R. R. Tolkien, and Charles Williams.* Carbondale: Southern Illinois University Press, 1969.

HOBANA, ION *Imaginile posibilului filmul stiintifico-fantastic.* Bucuresti: Editura Meridiane, 1968.

HOBANA, ION (ed.) *Viitorul a început ieri.* Bucuresti: Editura tineretului, 1966.

HOBANA, ION (ed.) *Viitorul? Atentie! Studii si articole despre literatura stiintifico-fantastica alese, adnotate, si comentate de Ion Hobana.* Bucuresti: Editura tineretului, 1968.

HORVÁTH, ARPÁD *Verne a technika álmodója.* Budapest: Táncsics, 1969.

HUSS, ROY AND T. J. ROSS (ed.) *Focus on the Horror Film.* Englewood Cliffs: Prentice Hall, 1972.

ISAACS, NEIL D. AND ROSE A. ZIMBARDO (ed.) *Tolkien and the Critics.* Notre Dame: University of Notre Dame, 1970.

JEHMLICH, REIMER and HARTMUT LÜCK (eds.) *Die deformierte Zukunft. Untersuchungen zur Science Fiction.* Munich: Goldmann Verlag, 1974.

JOHNSON, WILLIAM (ed.) *Focus on the Science Fiction Film.* Englewood Cliffs: Prentice Hall, 1972.

KAGARLITSKI, JULIUS *The Life and Thought of H. G. Wells.* London: Sidgwick and Jackson, 1966.

KAGARLITSKI, JULIUS *Chto takoie fantastika?* Moscow: Khudozhestvennaia literatura, 1974.

KAMLAH, WILHELM *Utopie, Eschatologie, Geschichtsteleologie. Kritische Untersuchungen zum Ursprung und zum futurischen Denken der Neuzeit.* Mannheim: Bibliographisches Institut, 1969.

KETTERER, DAVID *New Worlds for Old. The apocalyptic imagination, Science Fiction, and American literature.* New York: Anchor Press/Doubleday, 1974.

KLINKOWITZ, JEROME, and JOHN SOMER (ed.) *The Vonnegut Statement.* New York: Dell Publishing Co., 1973.

KNIGHT, DAMON *In Search of Wonder.* Chicago: Advent Publishers, 1956. Enlarged second edition, 1967.

KOCHER, PAUL H. *Master of Middle-Earth. The fiction of J. R. R. Tolkien.* Boston: Houghton Mifflin Co., 1972. London: Thames and Hudson, 1972.

KOLODYŃSKI, ANDRZEJ *Filmy fantastyczno-naukowe.* Warsaw: Wydawnictwa artystyczne i filmowe, 1972.

KRYSMANSKI, HANS-JURGEN *Die utopische Methode.* Köln and Opladen: Westdeutscher Verlag, 1963.

LARIN, S. *Literatura krylatoi mechty.* Moscow: Znanie, 1961.

LEINER, FRIEDRICH and JURGEN GUTSCH: *Science-fiction. Materialien und Hinweise.* Frankfurt/Main, Berlin, Munich: Verlag Moritz Diesterweg, 1972.

LEM, STANISŁAW *Fantastyka i futurologia.* Kraków: Wydawnictwo Literackie, 1970, 1973

LÉVY, MAURICE *Lovecraft.* Paris: Union Générale d'Editions, 1972.

LEWIS, C. S. *Of Other Worlds: Essays and Stories.* New York: Harcourt, Brace and World, 1966.

LIAPUNOV, BORIS *Aleksandr Beliaev.* Moscow: Sovetski pisatel', 1967.

LUNDWALL, SAM J. *Science Fiction från begynnelsen till våra dagar.* Stockholm: Sveriges Radios förlag, 1969.

LUNDWALL, SAM J. *Science Fiction: What It's All About.* New York: Ace Books, 1971.

LUPOFF, RICHARD A. *Edgar Rice Burroughs: Master of Adventure.* New York: Canaveral Press, 1965. New York: Ace Books, 1968.

LUPOFF, DICK and DON THOMPSON (ed.): *All in Color for a Dime.* Arlington House, 1970

MACKENZIE, NORMAN and JEANNE *H. G. Wells. A biography.* New York: Simon and Schuster, 1973.

MANUEL, FRANK E. (ed.) *Utopias and Utopian Thought.* Boston: Houghton Mifflin, 1966.

MODELMOG, ILSE *Die andere Zukunft. Zur utopischen Kommunikation.* Düsseldorf: Bertelsmann Universitätsverlag, 1970.

MOORE, PATRICK *Science and Fiction.* London: George Harrap, 1958.

MORÉ, MARCEL: *Nouvelles explorations de Verne, le problème du père dans les 'Voyages extraordinaires'.* Paris: Gallimard, 1960.

MORÉ, MARCEL: *Nouvelles explorations de Jules Verne. Musique Misgamic.* Paris: Gallimard, 1963.

MORTON, A. L. *The English Utopia.* London: Lawrence and Wishart, 1952.

MOSKOWITZ, SAM *Explorers of the Infinite: Shapers of Science Fiction.* Cleveland and New York: The World Publishing Co., 1963.

MOSKOWITZ, SAM *The Immortal Storm. A history of science fiction fandom.* Atlanta: The Atlanta Science Fiction Organization Press, 1954.

MOSKOWITZ, SAM *Science Fiction by Gaslight. A history and anthology of Science Fiction in the popular magazines, 1891–1911.* Cleveland and New York: The World Publishing Company, 1968.

MOSKOWITZ, SAM *Seekers of Tomorrow: Masters of Modern Science Fiction.* Cleveland and New York: World Publishing Co., 1966.

MOSKOWITZ, SAM *Under the Moons of Mars. A history and anthology of 'The Scientific Romance' in the Munsey magazines, 1912–20.* New York, Chicago, San Francisco: Holt, Rinehart and Winston, 1970.

NAGL, MANFRED *Science Fiction in Deutschland. Untersuchungen zur Genese, Soziographie und Ideologie der phantastischen Massenliteratur.* Tübinger Vereinigung für Volkskunde e. V., 1972.

NEUSUSS, ARNHELM (ed.) *Utopie. Begriff und Phänomen des Utopischen.* Neuwied and Berlin: Luchterhand, 1968.

NICOLSON, MARJORIE HOPE *Voyages to the Moon.* New York: Macmillan 1948, 1960.

NODA, MASAHIRO *SF Eiyugunzo.* Tokyo: Hayakawa shobo, 1968.

NODA, MASAHIRO *Uchuusen Yaro.* Tokyo: Akita shobo, 1969.

PAGETTI, CARLO *Il Senso del Futuro. La Fantascienza nella Letteratura Americana.* Roma: Edizioni di Storia e Letteratura, 1970.

PANSHIN, ALEXEI *Heinlein in Dimension.* Chicago: Advent Publishers, 1968.

PARNOV, E. *Sovremennaia nauchnaia fantastika.* Moscow: Znanie, 1968.

PARRINGTON, VERNON LOUIS, JR *American Dreams. A study of American utopias.* Providence: Brown University Press, 1974. Second edition, enlarged. New York: Russel and Russel, 1964.

PEHLKE, MICHAEL and NORBERT LINGFELD: *Roboter und Gartenlaube. Ideologie und Unterhaltung in der Science-Fiction-Literatur.* Munich: Carl Hanser Verlag, 1970.

PHILMUS, ROBERT M. *Into the Unknown: The Evolution of Science Fiction from Francis Godwin to H. G. Wells.* Berkeley: University of California Press, 1970.

PLANK, ROBERT: *The Emotional Significance of Imaginary Beings: A Study of the Interaction between Psychotherapy, Literature, and Reality in the Modern World.* Springfield (Illinois): Charles C. Thomas, 1968.

POPP, MAX *Julius Verne und sein Werk.* Wien und Leipzig: Hartleben, 1909.

RAKNEM, INGVALD *H. G. Wells and his Critics.* Oslo: Universitetsforlaget, 1962.

READY, WILLIAM *The Tolkien Relation. A personal inquiry.* Chicago: Henry Regnery Company, 1968.

REED, PETER J. *Kurt Vonnegut, Jr.* New York: Warner Paperback Library, 1972.

RIHA, KARL *Zak, roarr wumm. Zur Geschichte der Comics-Literatur.* Steinbach: Anabas Verlag, 1970.

RIURIKOV, IU. *Cherez 100 i 1000 let.* Moscow: Iskusstvo, 1961.

ROGERS, ALVA *A Requiem for Astounding.* Chicago: Advent Publishers, 1964.

ROSE, LOIS and STEPHEN *The Shattered Ring. Science Fiction and the quest for meaning.* Richmond, Virginia: John Knox Press, 1970.

ROTTENSTEINER, FRANZ (ed.) *Insel Almanach auf das Jahr 1972.* Frankfurt/Main: Insel Verlag, 1971.

ROTTENSTEINER FRANZ (ed.) *Polaris I. Ein Science-Fiction-Almanach.* Frankfurt/Main: Insel Verlag, 1973.

ROTTENSTEINER, FRANZ (ed.) *Polaris II. Ein Science-Fiction-Almanach.* Frankfurt/Main: Insel Verlag, 1974.

RUOSCH, CHRISTIAN *Die phantastisch-surreale Welt im Werke Paul Scheerbarts.* Bern: Verlag Herbert Lang and Cie, 1970

SADOUL, JACQUES *Histoire de la Science Science Fiction. Eine Untersuchung über* 1973.

SCHWONKE, MARTIN *Vom Staatsroman zur Science Fiction. Eine Untersuchung über Geschichte und Funktion der naturwissenschaftlichtechnischen Utopie.* Stuttgart: Ferdinand Enke Verlag, 1957.

SERVIER, JEAN *Histoire de l'utopie.* Paris: Gallimard, 1967.

SILVERBERG, ROBERT (ed.) *The Mirror of Infinity. A critics' anthology of Science Fiction.* New York: Harper and Row, 1970

SOLMI, SERGIO *Della Favola, del Viaggio e di altre cose* (Saggi sul Fantastico). Milano: Editore Riccardo Ricciardi, 1971.

STERNBERG, JACQUES *Une succursale du fantastique nommée Science-fiction.* Paris: 'Le Terrain Vague', 1958.

STOVER, LEON: *La Science Fiction Américaine.* Paris: Editions Aubier Montaigne, 1972.

SUVIN, DARKO *Od Lukijana do Lunjika.* Zagreb: Epoha, 1965.

SUVIN, DARKO (ed.) *Other Worlds, Other Seas: Science Fiction stories from socialist countries.* New York: Random House, 1970.

SWAHN, SVEN CHRISTER *7 by framtiden.* Malmö: Bernces Förlag, 1974.

TUZINSKI, KONRAD *Das Individuum in der englischen devolutionistischen Utopie.* Tübingen: Max Niemeyer Verlag, 1965.

URBAN, ADOL'F *Fantastika i nash mir.* Leningrad: Sovetski pisatel', 1972.

VAN HERP, JACQUES *Panorama de la Science Fiction.* Verviers: André Gerard (Marabout), 1973.

VAX, LOUIS *L'art et la littérature fantastiques.* Paris: Presses Universitaires de France, 1970.

VAX, LOUIS *La séduction de l'étrange.* Paris: Presses Universitaires de France, 1965.

VILLGRADTER, RUDOLF and FRIEDRICH KREY (ed.) *Der utopische Roman.* Darmstadt: Wissenschaftliche Buchgesellschaft, 1973.

Vom Geist der Superhelden. Comic Strips. Colloquium zur Theorie der Bildergeschichte in der Akademie der Künste Berlin. Berlin: Geb. Mann Verlag, 1970.

WALSH, CHAD *From Utopia to Nightmare.* New York: Harper and Row, 1962.

WARNER, HARRY, JR *All Our Yesterdays.* Chicago: Advent Publishers, 1969.

WERTHAM, FREDERIC *The World of Fanzines. A special form of communication.* Carbondale and Edwardsville: Southern Illinois University Press, 1973.

WHITFIELD, STEPHEN E. and GENE RODDENBERRY *The Making of Star Trek*. New York: Ballantine Books, 1968.

WILLIAMSON, JACK *H. G. Wells: Critic of Progress*. Baltimore: The Mirage Press, 1973.

WILSON, ROBIN SCOTT (ed.) *Those Who Can: A Science Fiction Reader*. New York: New American Library, 1973.

WOLLHEIM, DONALD A. *The Universe Makers: Science Fiction Today*. New York: Harper and Row, 1971.

YERSHOV, PETER *Science Fiction and Utopian Fantasy in Soviet Literature*. New York: Research Program on the U.S.S.R., 1954.

ZACHARASIEWICZ, WALDEMAR *Die 'Cosmic Voyage' und die 'Excursion' in der englischen Dichtung des 17. und 18. Jahrhunderts*. Wien: Verlag Notring, 1969.

Academic periodicals on science fiction

Extrapolation. Thomas D. Clareson, Box 3186, The College of Wooster, Wooster, Ohio 44691.

Foundation. The Science Fiction Foundation, North East London Polytechnic, Longbridge Road, Essex RM8 2AS, England.

Science-Fiction Studies. Department of English, Indiana State University, Terre Haute, Indiana 47809.

Recommended amateur periodicals ('fanzines'):

The Alien Critic. Richard E. Geis, Box 11408, Portland, Ore. 97211.

Algol. Andrew Porter, PO Box 4175, New York, N.Y. 10017.

Locus. Charles and Dena Brown, Box 3938, San Francisco, CA 94119. The news magazine of the sf field, twice a month.

Luna Monthly. Frank and Ann Dietz, 655 Orchard Street, Oradell, N.J. 07649, International sf news, reviews and bibliographies.

Riverside Quarterly. Leland Sapiro, Box 14451 University Station, Gainesville, Fl. 32604.

SF Commentary. Bruce R. Gillespie, GPO Box 51955A Melbourne, Victoria 3001, Australia.

Science Fiction Times. Hans-Joachim Alpers, D-285 Bremerhaven 1, Weissenburger Str. 6, Western Germany (in German).

Speculation. Peter R. Weston, 72 Beeches Drive, Erdington, Birmingham RQ4 0DT.

Vector. The Journal of the British Science Fiction Association. Malcom Edwards, 75A Harrow View, Middx HA1 1RF,

United Kingdom.

Issues of general periodicals devoted in part or entirely to science fiction:

L'Arc No. 29, 1966 (in French, Jules Verne).

Argument No. 9, 1958 (in French).

Arts in Society No. 2, Summer/Fall 1969.

Les Cahiers de L'Herne 1969 (in French, Lovecraft issue).

Les Cahiers du Sud No. 317, 1953 (French).

Critique Vol. XII, No. 3, 1971 (Kurt Vonnegut, Jr).

Daedalus 94, Spring 1965 (on utopias).

Edge No. 5/6, Autumn/Winter 1973 (New Zealand).

Esprit May 1953 (in French).

Esprit No. 2, 1966 (in French; on utopias).

Europe No. 139–140, July–August 1957 (in French).

Helikon Vol. XVIII, No. 1, 1972 (in Hungarian).

The Journal of Popular Culture Spring 1972.

Littérature December 1972 (in French).

Nurt No. 8, 1972 (in Polish; on Stanislaw Lem).

O fantastike i prikliucheniiakh – O literature dlia detei No. 5, 1960 (in Russian).

Revue des Belles-Lettres No. 4, 1955 (in French, Switzerland).

Romanian Review Vol. XXII, No. 1, 1969.

The Shaw Review Vol. XVI, No. 2, May 1973.

Soviet Literature No. 5, 1968.

Sozialistische Zeitschrift für Kunst und Gesellschaft No. 18/19, July 1973 (in German).

Studies in the Literary Imagination Fall 1973.

Il Subbio. Arte e Letteratura di Scienze Fiction, 1972 (in Italian).

Summary No. 1, 1971 (Kurt Vonnegut, Jr).

Le Table Ronde No. 85, January 1955 (in French).

Tribuna Vol. XVII, No. 51, December 20, 1973 (in Rumanian).

Uj Irás September 1967 (in Hungarian).

Viata Românească Vol. XXVII, No. 1, January 1974 (in Rumanian).

Nebula Awards

The Nebula Awards are commendations made annually since 1965 by the Science Fiction Writers of America for outstanding achievements in the field of sf.

1965

Best Novel: *Dune* by Frank Herbert
Best Novella: (tie) *The Saliva Tree* by Brian W. Aldiss
He Who Shapes by Roger Zelazny

Best Novelette: *The Doors of His Face, the Lamps of His Mouth* by Roger Zelazny
Best Short Story: ' "Repent, Harlequin!" Said the Ticktockman' by Harlan Ellison

1966

Best Novel: (tie) *Flowers for Algernon* by Daniel Keyes
Babel 17 by Samuel R. Delany
Best Novella: *The Last Castle* by Jack Vance
Best Novelette: *Call Him Lord* by Gordon R. Dickson
Best Short Story: 'The Secret Place' by Richard Mackenna

1967

Best Novel: *The Einstein Intersection* by Samuel R. Delany
Best Novella: *Behold the Man* by Michael Moorcock
Best Novelette: *Gonna Roll the Bones* by Fritz Leiber
Best Short Story: 'Aye, and Gomorrah' by Samuel R. Delany

1968

Best Novel: *Rite of Passage* by Alexei Panshin
Best Novella: *Dragonrider* by Anne McCaffrey
Best Novelette: *Mother to the World* by Richard Wilson
Best Short Story: 'The Planners' by Kate Wilhelm

1969

Best Novel: *The Left Hand of Darkness* by Ursula K. Le Guin
Best Novella: *A Boy and His Dog* by Harlan Ellison
Best Novelette: *Time Considered as a Helix of Semi-Precious Stones* by Samuel R. Delany
Best Short Story: 'Passengers' by Robert Silverberg

1970

Best Novel: *Ringworld* by Larry Niven
Best Novella: *Ill Met in Lankhmar* by Fritz Leiber
Best Novelette: *Slow Sculpture* by Theodore Sturgeon
Best Short Story: No Award

1971

Best Novel: *A Time of Changes* by Robert Silverberg
Best Novella: *The Missing Man* by Katherine Maclean
Best Novelette: *The Queen of Air and Darkness* by Poul Anderson

Best Short Story: 'Good News from the Vatican' by Robert Silverberg

1972

Best Novel: *The Gods Themselves* by Isaac Asimov

Best Novella: *A Meeting With Medusa* by Arthur C. Clarke

Best Novelette: *Goat Song* by Poul Anderson

Best Short Story: 'When It Changed' by Joanna Russ

1973

Best Novel: *Rendezvous with Rama* by Arthur C. Clarke

Best Novella: *The Death of Dr Island* by Gene Wolfe

Best Novelette: *Of Mist, and Grass, and Sand* by Vonda McIntyre

Best Short Story: 'Love is the Plan, the Plan is Death' by James Tiptree, Jr

Best Dramatic Presentation: *Soylent Green*

Hugo Awards

The Hugo Awards are presented annually by the World Science Fiction Conventions for outstanding achievement in the field of sf.

1953 – 11th Convention – Philadelphia:

No. 1 Fan Personality: Forrest J. Ackerman

Interior Illustrator: Virgil Finlay

Cover Artist: Ed Emshwiller and Hannes Bok (tie)

Excellence in Fact Articles: Willy Ley

New Science Fiction Author or Artist: Philip José Farmer

Professional Magazine: *Galaxy* and *Astounding Science Fiction*

Novel: *The Demolished Man* by Alfred Bester

1954 – 12th Convention – San Francisco:

No awards were given this year.

1955 – 13th Convention – Cleveland:

Novel: *They'd Rather Be Right* by Mark Clifton and Frank Riley

Novelette: *The Darfsteller* by Walter M. Miller, Jr

Short Story: 'Allamagoosa' by Eric Frank Russell

Professional Magazine: *Astounding Science Fiction*

Illustrator: Frank Kelly Freas

Amateur Publication: *Fantasy Times*, James V. Taurasi, ed.

1956 – 14th Convention – New York:

Novel: *Double Star* by Robert A. Heinlein

Novelette: *Exploration Team* by Murray Leinster

Short Story: 'The Star' by Arthur C. Clarke

Feature Writer: Willy Ley

Professional Magazine: *Astounding Science Fiction*

Illustrator: Frank Kelly Freas

Amateur Publication: *Inside and Science Fiction Advertiser*, Ron Smith, ed.

Critic: Damon Knight

1957 – 15th Convention – London:

Professional Magazine, American: *Astounding Science Fiction*

Professional Magazine, British: *New Worlds Science Fiction*

Amateur Publication: *Science Fiction Times*, James V. Taurasi, ed.

1958 – 16th Convention – Los Angeles:

Novel: *The Big Time* by Fritz Leiber

Short Story: 'Or All The Seas With Oysters' by Avram Davidson

Professional Magazine: *Magazine of Fantasy and Science Fiction*

Illustrator: Frank Kelly Freas

Motion Picture: *The Incredible Shrinking Man*

Most Outstanding Actifan: Walter A. Willis

1959 – 17th Convention – Detroit:

Novel: *A Case of Conscience* by James Blish

Novelette: *The Big Front Yard* by Clifford D. Simak

Short Story: 'The Hell-Bound Train' by Robert Bloch

Illustrator: Frank Kelly Freas

Professional Magazine: *Magazine of Fantasy and Science Fiction*

Amateur Publication: *Fanac*, Terry Carr and Ron Ellik, eds.

Most Promising New Author: Brian W. Aldiss

1960 – 18th Convention – Pittsburgh:

Novel: *Starship Trooper* by Robert A. Heinlein

Short Fiction: *Flowers For Algernon* by Daniel Keyes

Professional Magazine: *Magazine of Fantasy and Science Fiction*

Amateur Publication: *Cry of the Nameless*, F. M. Busby, ed.

Illustrator: Ed Emshwiller

Dramatic Presentation: *The Twilight Zone* by Rod Serling

Special Award: To Hugo Gernsback as 'The Father of Magazine Science Fiction'

1961 – 19th Convention – Seattle:

Novel: *A Canticle for Leibowitz* by Walter M. Miller, Jr

Short Story: 'The Longest Voyage' by Poul Anderson

Professional Magazine: *Analog*

Amateur Publication: *Who Killed Science Fiction?* Earl Kemp, ed.

Illustrator: Ed Emshwiller

Dramatic Presentation: *The Twilight Zone* by Rod Serling

1962 – 20th Convention – Chicago:

Novel: *Stranger in a Strange Land* by Robert A. Heinlein

Short Fiction: *The Hothouse Series* by Brian W. Aldiss

Professional Magazine: *Analog*

Amateur Magazine: *Warhoon*, Richard Bergeron, ed.

Professional Artist: Ed Emshwiller

Dramatic Presentation: *The Twilight Zone* by Rod Serling

1963 – 21st Convention – Washington D.C.:

Novel: *The Man in the High Castle* by Philip K. Dick

Short Fiction: *The Dragon Masters* by Jack Vance

Dramatic Award: No award

Professional Magazine: *Magazine of Fantasy and Science Fiction*

Amateur Magazine: *Xero*, Dick Lupoff, ed.

Professional Artist: Roy Krenkel

Special Awards: P. Schuyler Miller (for Best Book Reviews)

Isaac Asimov (Distinguished Contributions To The Field)

1964 – 22nd Convention – Oakland:

Novel: *Way Station* by Clifford Simak

Short Fiction: *No Truce With Kings* by Poul Anderson

Professional Magazine: *Analog*

Professional Artist: Ed Emshwiller

Book Publisher: Ace Books

Amateur Publication: *Amra*, George Scithers, ed.

1965 – 23rd Convention – London:

Novel: *The Wanderer* by Fritz Leiber

Short Fiction: *Soldier, Ask Not* by Gordon Dickson

Professional Magazine: *Analog*

Professional Artist: John Schoenherr

Book Publisher: Ballantine Books

Amateur Publication: *Yandro*, Robert and Juanita Coulson, eds.

Dramatic Presentation: *Dr Strangelove*

1966 – 24th Convention – Cleveland:

Novel: (tie) *And Call Me Conrad* by

Roger Zelazny
Dune by Frank Herbert
Short Fiction: '"Repent, Harlequin!"
Said the Ticktockman' by Harlan Ellison
Professional Magazine: If
Professional Artist: Frank Frazetta
Amateur Magazine: ERB-dom, Camille
Cazedessus, Jr, ed.
Best All-Time Series: Foundation Series
by Isaac Asimov

1967 – 25th Convention – New York:

Novel: The Moon Is a Harsh Mistress by
Robert A. Heinlein
Novelette: The Last Castle by Jack Vance
Short Story: 'Neutron Star' by Larry
Niven
Professional Magazine: If
Professional Artist: Jack Gaughan
Dramatic Presentation: 'The Menagerie'
(Star Trek)
Amateur Publication: Niekas, Ed Meskys
and Felice Rolfe, eds.
Fan Artist: Jack Gaughan
Fan Writer: Alexei Panshin

1968 – 26th Convention – Oakland:

Novel: Lord of Light by Roger Zelazny
Novella: (tie) Weyr Search by Ann
McCaffrey
Riders of the Purple Wage by Philip José
Farmer
Novelette: Gonna Roll the Bones by
Fritz Leiber
Short Story: 'I Have No Mouth and I
Must Scream' by Harlan Ellison
Dramatic Presentation: 'City on the Edge
of Forever' by Harlan Ellison (Star
Trek)
Professional Magazine: If
Professional Artist: Jack Gaughan
Amateur Publication: Amra, George
Scithers, ed.
Fan Artist: George Barr
Fan Writer: Ted White

1969 – 27th Convention – St Louis:

Novel: Stand on Zanzibar by John Brunner
Novella: Nightwings by Robert Silverberg
Novelette: The Sharing of Flesh by Poul
Anderson
Short Story: 'The Beast that Shouted
Love at the Heart of the World' by
Harlan Ellison
Dramatic Presentation: 2001: A Space
Odyssey by Arthur C. Clarke
Professional Magazine: The Magazine of
Fantasy and Science Fiction
Professional Artist: Jack Gaughan
Fan Artist: Vaughn Bode
Fanzine: Psychotic
Fan Writer: Harry Warner, Jr
Special Award: Armstrong, Aldrin, and
Collins for 'the best moon landing ever'

1970 – 28th Convention – Heidelberg:

Novel: The Left Hand of Darkness by
Ursula K. Le Guin
Novella: Ship of Shadows by Fritz Leiber
Short Story: 'Time Considered as a Helix
of Semi-Precious Stones' by Samuel
R. Delany
Dramatic Presentation: TV coverage of
Apollo XI
Professional Magazine: The Magazine of
Fantasy and Science Fiction
Professional Artist: Frank Kelly Freas
Fan Magazine: Science Fiction Review
Fan Writer: Bob Tucker
Fan Artist: Tim Kirk

1971 – 29th Convention – Boston:

Novel: Ringworld by Larry Niven
Novella: Ill Met in Lankhmar by Fritz
Leiber
Short Story: 'Slow Sculpture' by Theodore
Sturgeon
Dramatic Presentation: No Award
Professional Magazine: The Magazine of
Fantasy and Science Fiction
Professional Artist: Leo and Diane Dillon
Fanzine: Locus
Fan: Alicia Austin
Fan writer: Richard Geis

1972 – 30th Convention – Los Angeles:

Novel: To Your Scattered Bodies Go by
Philip José Farmer
Novella: The Queen of Air and Darkness
by Poul Anderson
Short Story: 'Inconstant Moon' by Larry
Niven
Dramatic Presentation: A Clockwork
Orange
Professional Magazine: The Magazine of
Fantasy and Science Fiction
Amateur Magazine: Locus
Professional Artist: Frank Kelly Freas
Fan Artist: Tim Kirk
Fan Writer: Harry Warner, Jr

1973 – 31st Convention – Toronto:

Novel: The Gods Themselves by Isaac
Asimov
Novella: The Word for World Is Forest
by Ursula K. Le Guin
Novelette: Goat Song by Poul Anderson
Short Story: (tie) 'The Meeting' by
Frederik Pohl and C. M. Kornbluth
'Eurem's Dam' by R. A. Lafferty
Professional Artist: Frank Kelly Freas
Professional Editor: Ben Bova (Analog)
Dramatic Presentation: Slaughterhouse
Five
Amateur Magazine: Energumen
Fan Artist: Tim Kirk
Fan Writer: Terry Carr

1974 – 32nd Convention
Novel: Rendezvous with Rama by Arthur
C. Clarke
Novella: The Girl Who Was Plugged In by
James Tiptree, Jr
Novelette: The Deathbird by Harlan Ellison
Short Story: 'The Ones Who Walk Away
from Omelas' by Ursula K. Le Guin
Professional Editor: Ben Bova
Fanzine: (tie) Algol and The Alien Critic
Professional Artist: Frank Kelly Freas
Dramatic Presentation: Sleeper (Woody
Allen)
Fan Writer: Susan Glicksohn
Fan Artist: Tim Kirk

The illustrations used in this book have
been provided from the author's own
archives with the following exceptions:
film stills on the pages indicated were
supplied by the following. 5, 35, 86
Hammer Films; 8, 10, 24–25, 33, 35, 53,
73, 74, 79, 80–81, 86, 87, 92, 100, 102,
125, 128, 129, 139, 140, 142, 147 National
Film Archive; 14, 18, 19, 20, 23, 36, 76,
83 The Museum of Modern Art Film
Stills Archive; 18 United Artists Corporation; 28, 29, 139 Springer/Bettmann
Film Archive; 67, 68–69 Buena Vista
Film Distribution Company; 72–73, 138–
139 Edwin Smith; 90–91, 92 Stanley
Kubrick/Warner Bros.; 97 American
International Pictures; 102 Universal
Pictures; 119, 121 B.B.C.